VOLUME

3

THE
AMERICAN HERITAGE
BOOK OF THE
PRESIDENTS
AND FAMOUS AMERICANS

★ ★ ★ ★ ★

JOHN QUINCY ADAMS

ANDREW JACKSON

MARTIN VAN BUREN

CREATED AND DESIGNED BY THE EDITORS OF
AMERICAN HERITAGE
The Magazine of History

12-VOLUME EDITION PUBLISHED BY
DELL PUBLISHING CO., INC., NEW YORK, N.Y.

John Quincy Adams

Andrew Jackson

Martin Van Buren

CONTENTS
OF VOLUME THREE

FAMOUS AMERICANS

JOHN QUINCY ADAMS

Of the second Adams-Jackson contest for the Presidency, historian Edward Channing wrote, ". . . it was more honorable to have been defeated in 1828 than to have been elected." The recipient of the honor was John Quincy Adams, by his own admission a man of impeccable character, who during the mucky campaign was charged with having entered into a "corrupt bargain." Self-defense or countercharge was out of the question: refusing to sink to the level of his opponents, Adams remained tight-lipped, retained his dignity, and was soundly beaten. "The sun of my political life," he confided to his diary, "sets in the deepest gloom."

His political sun was in fact not ready to set. Before he achieved the Presidency, Adams had compiled a substantial record of service to his state and country—a record that for one other than an Adams might have represented the work of two lifetimes. But he was an Adams, and as such, work and service were almost instinctive. Though sixty-one when he left the White House, he soon began his career anew: for the last eighteen years of his life he sat, stood, debated, and fought in the House of Representatives, where he came to be known as Old Man Eloquent, one of the ablest and most effective congressmen of his or later days.

The second child and first son of John and Abigail Adams, he was born in Braintree, Massachusetts, on July 11, 1767. When John Quincy was three, his father temporarily retired from politics, and as his re-entrance was gradual, John Adams was home often enough to establish an extremely close if not demonstrative relationship with his son. With the Revolution in the making, the precocious John Quincy Adams was quite receptive to his father's anti-British sentiments and explanations of the issues. Before he was seven he had become a faithful reader of the patriot press, and when with his mother he

*Gilbert Stuart began the portrait of Adams
at left; it was completed by Thomas Sully.*

witnessed the Battle of Bunker Hill in 1775, he saw testament to all he had read and heard; he remained biased against the English for life.

In 1778 and again the next year, John Quincy accompanied his father to Europe on diplomatic missions. Educated in Paris, Amsterdam, and Leyden, and by his father, the youth developed sophisticated interests, ranging from history to agriculture, from economics to gastronomy. In many respects these years marked the end of childhood; one hesitates to call the teen-aged John Quincy Adams anything less than a mature adult. Even his strongly opinionated father allowed him to make his own decisions. In 1781, at the age of fourteen, John Quincy was invited to leave school to go to St. Petersburg to serve as private secretary to Francis Dana, American minister to Russia. Despite his age, young Adams was a valuable aid to the consul; he enjoyed Russia and the exposure to diplomatic circles. After a year, however, displaying an extraordinary objectivity about himself, he decided it would be best for him to return to his studies in the Netherlands.

Slowed by the Scandinavian and North German winter, the journey to The Hague took six months, during which John Adams was largely uninformed about his son's whereabouts. No sooner had John Quincy settled down with his books when his father appeared and removed him to Paris, where he could keep a closer eye on him. There John Quincy watched the signing of the Treaty of Paris, ending the American Revolution, and held his own in discussions with Franklin, Jay, Jefferson, his father of course, and whomever else he encountered, American or foreign, in several languages.

John Adams was sent to London in 1785, and John Quincy—again on his own—decided he had better get on with his education, this time without distractions. He returned to the United States and enrolled at Harvard. Understandably, after his experiences abroad, he found college life dull, but he graduated in two years and entered the law offices of Theophilus Parsons in New-

John Quincy Adams, sketched when he was sixteen

buryport, Massachusetts. Passing the bar in 1790, he set up practice in Boston, though he had no intention of spending his life as a lawyer. But since his father was by then Vice President of the United States, John Quincy worried about charges of nepotism and was overcautious about entering governmental service.

For four years John Quincy Adams was one of the most prolific political writers in America. Most of his articles were defenses of the Washington administration, and the President was impressed. In 1794, George Washington dismissed the Adamses' reservations and appointed John Quincy minister to the Netherlands. During his three years at The Hague, Adams was twice called to London to help negotiate John Jay's treaty; there he met and courted Louisa Catherine Johnson, daughter of the Maryland-born American consul. Louisa had been born and raised in Europe and had in fact never seen the United States. They were married in July, 1797, a few months after John Adams had been inaugurated in Philadelphia as the second President of the United States.

The sensitive Adams wanted to appoint John Quincy minister to Prussia, but again he hesitated. Finally, however, he named his son to the post, but not before securing a strong endorsement from George Washington, who wrote from Mount Vernon that the President had no right to deny the country the services of John Quincy Adams just because he was an Adams, and added that he "will prove himself to be the ablest of all our diplomatic corps." The difficulty of the assignment was illustrated to the couple even before they entered Berlin. As recorded in Adams' diary, he and Louisa arrived at the gates to the city and were there detained "by a dapper lieutenant who did not know, until one of his private soldiers explained to him, who the United States of America were." Although many of his duties were routine, Adams did manage to conclude a treaty of commerce and friendship, and his stay, if uneventful, was regarded at home as successful. In 1801, however, shortly before his departure from office, the President recalled his son. It is possible that Adams wanted to dramatize the cleavage between himself and his successor, or that he wanted to spare Jefferson the embarrassment of having an Adams in his service; but although his motives have never been clearly defined, it is perhaps most likely that Adams, knowing that the new President would in fact retain the valuable John Quincy, could not bear the thought of being indebted to Jefferson for anything. In any case, the young Adams arrived home in the autumn of 1801 and soon re-opened his Boston law office.

But being an Adams meant that John Quincy belonged in public service. It meant that he was a statesman, not a politician, and as such it meant that he followed a carefully delineated set of rules—all his own—for statesmanly conduct. It meant that membership in a political party was a convenience—nothing more—and that his being a Federalist would make him no more predictable than his election by a constituency would make him faithful to its interests. In

John Adams wrote the letter at right, introducing his first son to the American minister in London.

April, 1802, forty-eight hours after he took his seat in the upper chamber of the Massachusetts legislature, the Federalists who had elected him began to question the wisdom of their choice: Adams voted in favor of giving the opposition Democratic-Republican minority a proportionate voice in that chamber. He pursued his independent ways as a United States senator between 1803 and 1808, voting for the Louisiana Purchase, which his party opposed, and for Jefferson's Embargo Act of 1807, although passage was regarded as disastrous to New England commerce. However often he voted with the Republicans he was not one of them: he bore no affection for the man in the White House and accused Jefferson of taking credit for being an economizer when in fact his economic measures were wasteful of "national safety, of national honour, of national glory. . . ."

Under persistent attack from all sides, Adams noted in his diary that when independence is besieged, "The qualities of mind most peculiarly called for are firmness, perseverance, patience, coolness, and forbearance." He did not have to acquire these traits; he had inherited them. Reserved, moral, able to labor twice beyond ordinary human exhaustion, vain one day and self-abusive the next, devotion to country un-

concealed by a transparent air of detachment, self-righteous, irritable, compelled to write, possessed with a firmness of purpose fluctuating between virtuous determination and stubborn inflexibility—this was the Adams character, fused in the father, solidified in the son. Moreover, to even a greater extent than his father, John Quincy Adams was practically paranoid about the family name. It was inconceivable to him that anyone might oppose him on reasonable grounds; his adversaries were out to get the Adamses, of that he was sure. Fortunately, he restricted most of his personal rantings to his diary, which in parts reads like a drama cast with the damned and set in hell. (In 1835, for example, he listed thirteen men, including a former ally or two, whose entire faculties, he said, were devoted to "base and dirty tricks to thwart my progress in life.")

After three years the Federalist-dominated Massachusetts legislature had had enough of Senator Adams' independence and symbolically censured him by electing a successor to his seat nine months in advance of the March, 1809, expiration date. Adams immediately resigned in a huff, thereby essentially ending his affiliation with the Federalist party. He retired to Cambridge, where three years earlier, in 1805, he had been appointed Boylston Professor of Rhetoric and Oratory at Harvard. Although he still yearned for a political career, his star was dim indeed. His record offended most New Englanders, and his anti-British bias was not then widely shared (it would take the War of 1812 to restore him to good graces on this point). Like

Adams always kept these small bronze busts of classical writers and philosophers on his mantelpiece.

his father, he found himself a man without a party and without a political base; but his father, at least, had waited until he was President before driving away support. Adams found himself futureless at forty-one.

It was James Madison, two days after his inauguration in March, 1809, who rescued the political career of John Quincy Adams by appointing him minister to Russia. He arrived in St. Petersburg in October and became a friend and confidant to Czar Alexander I. Two years later he received word that the President had appointed him to the Supreme Court. Much to his surprise the Senate had unanimously confirmed the appointment; but with characteristic objectivity Adams regarded himself as unfit for the judiciary and declined. Though there is no evidence to suggest that Adams regretted turning down the offer, he was before long eager to return to America. The War of 1812 was being fought at home, and the Russians were busy with Napoleon; Adams felt out of touch with the big events. In 1814, however, Madison asked him to leave Russia not for home but for Ghent, Belgium, where he and four other American commissioners were to try to conclude a peace with England. A treaty was signed on December 21, 1814, but not before seven miserable months had passed, not before Adams' dislike of the British had been countless times confirmed, and not before he riled and was, in turn, countless times riled by his fellow bargainer Henry Clay.

Then Adams was asked to go to London as minister to the Court of St. James's. The wisdom of appointing an anti-English consul to represent America immediately after a British-American conflict may be questioned, but Adams went. He had about as much success with the Crown as his father had had in the same position following the Revolution: very little. Besides, England, too, was busy with Napoleon, and Adams' duties were again rather routine. On April 16, 1817, he received notice to set sail as soon as possible; President James Monroe had appointed him Secretary of State.

To comprehend the breadth of Adams' accomplishments as Secretary of State, one need not look any further than to the overall record of the Monroe administration. It was the Adams-Onís Treaty of 1819 that added Spanish Florida to the United States. It was Adams who settled the Canada-United States border controversy in negotiations with England, and it was Adams' firmness that convinced the Russians not to go ahead with their plans to penetrate the Pacific Coast of North America. Most notably, when the President included in a State of the Union address the key phrase that became the Monroe Doctrine, it was Adams' policy, word for word, that he read. While there have been a number of Presidents who have taken exclusive control of policy-making, employing their Cabinet members merely as agents or pawns, Monroe was one who believed strongly in delegating responsibility. His greatest skill was that of an administrator, and as such he was a master at the art of choosing, rejecting, and distilling various contributions in order to assemble his own, no less personal, policy. The prevailing issue of his two terms was national expansion, which shaped all the smaller issues, domestic and foreign, and which made the State Department what it had not been before: a hub

Secretary of State Adams gave a ball for Andrew Jackson on January 8, 1824, the anniversary of the Battle of New Orleans. The men shown (from left to right) are John Calhoun, Daniel Webster, General Jackson, Henry Clay, and John Quincy Adams.

around which all the now-related issues revolved. Monroe was fortunate in having Adams as Secretary of State, and he knew it: that he chose to make Adams' policies his policies is indicative not of his lack of imagination but of his sound executive judgment.

Adams had been a fine diplomat, but his abruptness, which often came across as orneriness, had prevented him from becoming a great one. Now, as a statesman, Adams channeled his articulateness, inexhaustible energy, and creative intellect to his new responsibilities, and thanks to the paternal Monroe, who discreetly edited the cantankerousness from Adams' papers, he became a superb, perhaps matchless, Secretary of State. His day began at four thirty in the morning and seldom ended before eleven or

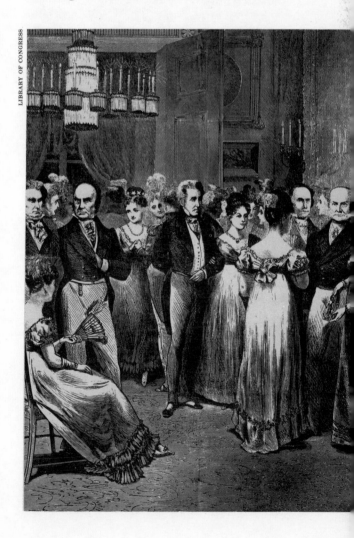

twelve at night, and the operations of his department went so smoothly that his labors were taken for granted. When Congress asked him to prepare a report on weights and measures, he agreed and produced a lengthy treatise, largely ignored in America, but applauded abroad, which is to this day widely regarded as one of the definitive expositions of the subject. Despite his feelings toward the British, his objectivity took priority over his prejudice, and he forged a series of alliances with England that planted once and for all the seeds of lasting friendship.

He wanted to be President, but although Adams was the most distinguished member of the Monroe Cabinet, his successes were somewhat neutralized by his lack of friends and organizational backing. There was only one party at the time—the Democratic-Republican—and a congressional caucus gave the presidential nomination to Secretary of the Treasury William H. Crawford of Georgia. This was not a popular choice in most states, and by election day, November 2, 1824, there were three other candidates: Senator Henry Clay, General Andrew Jackson, and Adams. Adams received his nomination from a New England that had long forgiven him and had come to view him as the man who would save the nation from the rabble-rousing "Old Hickory." Secretary of War John Calhoun, originally a presidential candidate, accepted the vice presidential nomination and became a supporter of Jackson. Calhoun won his race easily.

But none of the presidential candidates received a majority of electoral votes, so the election was placed in the hands of the House of Representatives. Because Jackson had led the balloting with 99 votes to Adams' 84, and had received over forty thousand more popular votes, his supporters claimed the House had no choice but to declare for the General. Clay, however, had been eliminated, finishing last with 37 votes despite the fact that Crawford, with four more, had suffered a paralytic stroke during the campaign. The election hinged on Clay's instructions to his small but devoted band of enthusiasts. After what must have been con-siderable soul-searching on his part, Clay endorsed his old adversary, Adams, and Adams won. The decision was not made official until three weeks before the inauguration.

When Adams announced that he had appointed Henry Clay Secretary of State, the Jackson-Calhoun forces cried foul. According to a Jacksonian newspaper, there had obviously been "a corrupt bargain." In Tennessee, Jackson's home, the legislature passed a resolution of condemnation: "Mr. Adams desired the office of President; he went into the combination without it, and came out with it. Mr. Clay desired that of Secretary of State; he went into the combination without it, and came out with it." Making the charges seem credible was the past relationship between the two men, which had been marked by petty personality clashes and general animosity. No evidence, then or since, has ever clarified the matter one way or the other; but even if there had been a deal, Clay had acted from conviction because he could have made the same arrangement with any candidate, and Adams, not one to rationalize, made it clear in his diary and personal correspondence that he thought Clay the best man for the job. Nevertheless, the charge of corruption echoed throughout

ADAMS NATIONAL HISTORIC SITE

Mrs. Adams used this china in the White House.

the Adams administration, branding it. It was hardly an administration at all.

What made the circumstances of Adams' Presidency doubly unfortunate for American history was the potential for greatness that the man exhibited. His character, capacity for work, statesmanship, and intellect were well-known; but in his first message to Congress, Adams revealed that he also had vision. Now that the vast expansion of the Monroe years had slowed and questionable border definitions were settled for the time being, Adams directed himself to the internal improvement of the country. His progressive program called for huge federal expenditures to establish an interstate network of roads and canals, a department of the interior to regulate use of natural resources, expeditions to map the country, a naval academy, a series of astronomical observatories, and government aid to education. Each provision, of course, did eventually become reality, but not in the Adams administration; it took Congress four years to debate and defeat each and every proposal.

The most vehement opposition came from the Jacksonians, who claimed that the President's plans placed too much power in the grip of the federal government. Yet, if passed, the program would actually have favored the common people for whom the Jacksonians expressed devotion. Development of the land and education of the people would have been expedited, thus providing "grass roots" Americans with the economic and intellectual strength to fight the Eastern, urban, big-money powers the Jacksonians so despised. Unfortunately, as Samuel Eliot Morison has pointed out, the Jacksonians, however significant their political accomplishments, did not always favor universal education. They sought support from whatever sources available, and if it was easier to appeal to the people's passions than to their minds, then forget education and condemn those who used it. The rise of the Jacksonians coincided with the rise of bigotry in the United States.

On the other hand, the anti-Jacksonians, who were beginning to call themselves Na-

A Creek chief, Selocta, wears a medal of President Adams in the portrait above. Beginning in 1827, the Creek were moved from Georgia to lands in the West.

tional Republicans, made no bones about their desire to limit suffrage to the moneyed and the educated. But, unlike the more aristocratic and now all but extinct Federalists, the National Republicans wanted that moneyed and educated class to eventually embrace all Americans. They opposed slavery and rallied behind President Adams' conscience-stricken plea for justice for the American Indian. Denouncing the "crying sins for which we are answerable before a higher jurisdiction," Adams wanted to provide the Indians with territory in the West and guarantee their rights there. But the more popular attitude was reflected in Jackson's treatment of the Indians in Florida—a blend of eviction and extermination—and Congress defeated the Adams plea. On issue after issue, the National Republican and Jacksonian wings drifted further apart, and two-party politics returned to the nation.

Adams wanted no part of it. He did not like partisan politics; he would not stoop to patronage; he would not make appointments on the basis of party affiliation. And when the partisan, highly regional issue of tariffs came up, Adams refused to take a stand, announcing that he would abide by the decision of Congress. So committed, when a bill creating an absurdly high tariff was passed and placed on his desk, he had no alternative but to sign, thereby losing what support he had in the South. Still, every previous President but one had won re-election, and in 1828 Adams was a candidate once again.

In his favor were the Chesapeake and Ohio Canal (one internal improvement for which Adams had been able to secure federal funds), a couple of commercial agreements with European countries, and the establishment of Pan-American rapport, as well as his character (if it could withstand the "corrupt bargain" charge) and a gracious First Lady presiding over social functions with such elegant restraint that almost nobody heard of them outside Washington. Against Adams were the corruption charges, his reputation for being antislavery and pro-Indian, a domestic program that was generally regarded as idiotic, a tariff that *was* idiotic, and an opponent who was the most popular military hero in America since George Washington, and who was backed by a well-organized machine that had been campaigning for four years. Naturally, Adams did not electioneer. Adamses serve but they do not campaign for office. Adamses also do not win second terms.

Nor do Adamses lose gracefully. Like his father, John Quincy Adams refused to attend the inauguration of his successor. Perhaps the younger Adams had better reason: he was beaten, his reputation muddied by a man he had once championed.

In 1830 the ex-President was elected Massachusetts delegate to the House of Representatives. He almost immediately displayed the old objectivity and even supported the position of President Jackson every now and then. He had not softened, though: he refused to attend when Jackson received an honorary degree from Harvard.

Always antislavery, Adams the congressman conducted a long, successful campaign to restore debate on abolition petitions, which had been halted by a "gag rule." On the grounds that it would extend slavery he opposed annexation of Texas. He was one of the few public figures who dared call the conflict with Mexico "a most unrighteous war." Instrumental in the establishment of the Smithsonian Institution, he also pressed for government provisions to make education available to all Americans. In 1843 the first observatory in America was finally established, and he was invited to lay the cornerstone on the hill site near Cincinnati that had been named Mount Adams.

In 1846 Adams suffered a paralytic stroke. Four months later he returned to the House, weak and with his speech impaired, and as he walked—with help—to his desk, the whole chamber rose and stood in homage. At that desk on February 21, 1848, he had another stroke. He was carried to the Speakers Room, where he remained until he died two days later. He regained consciousness only once. "Thank the officers of the House," he said. "This is the last of earth. I am content."

John Quincy Adams was not among America's more lovable figures, but he cared very deeply about the character of his people and country. He thought he knew what was best —often he did—for the nation that so frequently resisted him. But if he had had his way, he would have taken America by the hand and showed it the way, just as he had done with his six-year-old grandson, Henry Adams. In his third-person autobiography, Henry recalled: ". . . one summer morning [Henry had] a passionate outburst of rebellion against going to school . . . [when] the door of the President's library . . . opened, and the old man slowly came down. Putting on his hat, he took the boy's hand without a word, and walked with him, paralyzed by awe, up the road to the town . . . the boy reflected that an old gentleman close on eighty would never trouble himself to walk near a mile on a hot summer morning over a shadeless road to take a boy to school . . . but the old man did not stop, and the boy saw all his strategical points turned, one after another, until he found himself seated inside the school. . . . Not till then did the President release his hand and depart."

—DAVID JACOBS

John Quincy Adams

A PICTURE PORTFOLIO

A portrait of John Quincy Adams adorns this colorful sewing box, a campaign item in the hotly contested election of 1824.

Sliding down "ice hills," above, without sleds, was a popular activity in St. Petersburg during Adams' stay.

John Quincy Adams, as a neutral minister in St. Petersburg, was in an ideal position to watch the mobilization for the war between Russia and France. Above, Russian soldiers parade before the royal palace of Alexander I.

MINISTER TO RUSSIA

John Quincy Adams' success as minister to Russia saved him from the political scrap heap to which he had been relegated by those who deplored his disregard for party lines. He had already represented the United States at The Hague and in Prussia, where he had seen the rise of the tensions which beset Europe in the early 1800's. His mission in Russia was to urge freedom of the seas, to seek favorable treatment for American shipping in Russian waters, and to reaffirm the desire of the United States to avoid entanglement in continental policies. The Adamses arrived in St. Petersburg late in 1809 and soon were part of the capital's social whirl. (Adams grumbled, as had his father in Paris in the 1770's and 1780's, that such socializing wasted valuable time.) When fifty-two American ships were seized by Danish privateers, Adams appealed to Alexander I, who was eager for American friendship, to intercede. Through the Czar's efforts, the ships were released. By late 1810, Adams had convinced the Czar to discontinue the detainment of American ships (charged with carrying contraband) in Russian ports. The Czar's decision was in defiance of Napoleon's system of trade restrictions, and marked the beginning of the rapid deterioration of the Franco-Russian alliance. Open warfare between France and Russia began in 1812, one week after the outbreak of the Anglo-American conflict, which the Czar offered to mediate. Adams, who was later commended for his alacrity, immediately accepted the chance to end the war. But England refused the Czar's offer; she was winning the war and was deaf to offers of mediation on maritime issues. Peace would have to be negotiated directly, at Ghent.

Adams married European-born Louisa Johnson (above) in 1797. Her portrait is by Charles Bird King; John Singleton Copley painted Adams (below) in 1795, when the diplomat was twenty-eight.

The seal above was used at the signing of the Treaty of Ghent, and now is on display at the Adams National Historic Site in Quincy, Massachusetts. The city of Portsmouth, New Hampshire, was "in a perfect uproar of joy, shouts, illuminations, &c. &c." according to the broadside, below, that proclaims the end of the war.

PEACE!

Treaty of PEACE signed & arrived!

CENTINEL-OFFICE, Feb. 13, 6 o'cloch in the morning.

WE have this instant received in Thirty-two hours from N. York, the following

Great and Happy News!

To BENJAMIN RUSSELL, Esq. *Centinel-Office, Boston,*
New-York, Feb. 11, 1815.—Saturday Evening, 10 o'clock.

SIR—

I HASTEN to acquaint you, for the information of the Public, of the arrival here this afternoon of H. Br. Majesty's Sloop of War FAVORITE, in which has come passenger Mr. CARROLL, American Messenger, having in his possession a

TREATY OF PEACE

Between this Country and Great-Britain, signed on the 26th December last.

Mr. BAKER also is on board, as Agent for the British Government, the same who was formerly Charge de Affairs here.

Mr. Carroll reached town at eight o'clock this evening. He shewed to a friend of mine who is acquainted with him, the pacquet containing the Treaty, and a London Newspaper of the last date of December, announcing the signing of the *Treaty.*

It depends, however, as my friend observed, upon the act of the President to suspend hostilities on this side.

The gentlemen left London the 2d Jan. The *Transit* had sailed previously from a port on the Continent.

This city is in a perfect uproar of joy, shouts, illuminations, &c. &c.

I have undertaken to send you this by Express—the rider engaging to deliver it by *Eight o'clock on Monday morning.* The expense will be 225 dollars—If you can collect so much to indemnify me I will thank you so to do.

I am with respect, Sir, your obedient servant,

JONATHAN GOODHUE.

Printed at the Portsmouth Oracle-Office.

1815

MAKING A PEACE

The American delegation at Ghent faced many problems in addition to the demands of Britain's representatives. The war news during the summer of 1814 was depressing; and the growing threat of secession by New England Federalists weakened the American position at the conference table. And there were personality clashes within the United States delegation. John Quincy Adams found Henry Clay ir-

ritating, "dogmatical, over-bearing," and given to late hours and gambling. With typical candor, Adams acknowledged his own irascibility. He was annoyed when his drafts for the treaty were revised by his countrymen, but he admired James Bayard's "real self-command," and worked well with Albert Gallatin. At first, the British demanded that an Indian barrier territory be established between the United States and Canada, that the United States not fortify its Northern boundary, and that English navigation be permitted on the Mississippi. But by the end of 1814, England was increasingly concerned with European affairs and alarmed by American victories. She offered a peace which deferred many of the essential questions to further negotiation but which would at least end the fighting. On December 24, the Treaty of Ghent was signed.

Above, chief plenipotentiaries John Quincy Adams, center, and Lord Gambier conclude the Treaty of Ghent.

WILLIAM CRAWFORD

It is probable that only a series of paralyzing strokes in 1823 kept William Crawford from becoming the sixth President of the United States. The tall, handsome, engaging Southerner had served in the Senate since 1807, and had made many influential friends in Washington, yet he remained the maverick conservative he had been in the Georgia legislature. Basically a states' righter, he did advocate a moderate protective tariff and favored rechartering the National Bank. He was minister to France from 1813 to 1815; later, during Madison's second term as Chief Executive, he was Secretary of War and then of the Treasury. Declining to run for President in 1816, he was Monroe's Secretary of the Treasury for eight years, working effectively for internal improvements. His ambition and influence were strong, and he knew the power of patronage: "Crawford's Act" of 1820 limited the tenures of minor federal appointees to four years. In the free-for-all to succeed President Monroe, John Quincy Adams, Henry Clay, and Andrew Jackson all knew they had to beat Crawford, who had the support of Van Buren, Madison, and Jefferson. Then Crawford was stricken, and his nomination by a small congressional caucus was merely a gesture of respect and friendship. Winning only forty-one electoral votes, he ran a distant third in the race. Crawford then faded from national prominence. He died in 1834.

VICTORY AND DEFEAT

John Quincy Adams brought the office of Secretary of State to full flower under James Monroe. His firmness prevailed over the chicanery of Spanish minister Onís, and Spain gave up Florida and all claims to the Pacific Northwest. In dealing with Russia over Pacific Coast claims, Adams said in July of 1823, ". . . the American continents are no longer subjects for any new European colonial establishments." Five months later Monroe made that position a matter of doctrinaire policy.

Adams watched with distaste as men began to vie to succeed Monroe; he hated political manipulating and remained aloof: "I had neither talent nor inclination for intrigue." He was a man of old-fashioned ideals caught in a wave of new and seamy methods of competition. The virulence of the attacks on him during the close election of 1824 and following his appointment of Henry Clay as Secretary of State was only a prelude to what has been called Adams' "four years' martyrdom." Adams long had acknowledged that he was not a "popular man"; his personal and governmental ethics were in somber and stoical contrast to the Jacksonian democracy that was sweeping the nation. A solidly antiadministration Congress scrapped President Adams' vast domestic program, and he was ousted in the election of 1828. The acrimonious campaign left him embittered yet hopeful: "The cause of Union and of improvement will remain," Adams wrote in 1829. ". . . I have duties to it and to my country yet to discharge."

The cartoon above, drawn by David Claypoole Johnston in 1824, has Adams in the lead in the presidential race; William Crawford is just behind him, with Jackson third. An outdistanced Henry Clay scratches his head, at right. The drawing is rife with plays on words. "Hurra for our Jackson," shouts a supporter of Old Hickory, while John Adams cheers on "our son Jack."

"A FIG FOR THE
CONSTITUTION"

I bore some humble part in putting down the dynasty of John the First," shrilled John Randolph as John Quincy Adams was about to assume the Presidency. "I hope to aid in putting down the dynasty of John the Second," Adams, in turn, saw Randolph as the "superscription of a great man stamped upon base metal." Throughout his twenty-six years in Congress, Randolph never gave his opponents a respite; he was the unrelenting whip of the "Quids," the Old Republican element, and was an opponent of all legislation that threatened state sovereignty.

He was first elected to the House from his native Virginia in 1799, and soon became the Republican floor leader. But he split with Jefferson over the Louisiana Purchase and other questions. Rigid in his antifederalism, he was incensed that the administration was not, and he became leader of the conservative opposition. He hated Madison, says Irving Brant, because "peace with a man who outstripped him politically was no more possible to Randolph than marriage"—and Randolph was sexually impotent. He at first supported Monroe as Jefferson's successor, but later called Monroe a "Judas" for aligning himself with Madison. In discussing the moderate tariff of 1824, Randolph said ominously, "I do not stop to argue the constitutionality of this bill; I consider the Constitution a dead letter. . . . A fig for the Constitution . . . there is no magic in this word *union*." That year he promised to use "every . . . means short of actual insurrection" to block the passage of an internal improvements act.

Some saw Randolph as merely an obstructionist, while to others he was the most articulate champion of the fading states' rights cause. But all feared this enigma whose slashing wit often paid little heed to party lines. His rhetorical vitriol and flamboyant dress and manner (he often appeared in the House booted, spurred, and carrying a whip; he was a pistol brandisher, and his obscenity was notorious) bespoke a disturbed temperament and vanity. A fascinated contemporary described Randolph as "lean and sallow," with a small head and a face lined with "premature and unhealthy wrinkles." His limbs were "unnaturally . . . protracted. To his short and meager body are attached long legs which . . . grow larger as they approach the floor . . . giving his whole person the appearance of a sort of pyramid. His arms are the counterparts of his legs. . . ." Randolph was almost beardless; his voice was soprano. Manifestly brilliant and sensitive, he was deeply affected by his physiological misfortune. To a man who taunted him on his impotency, he retorted haughtily: "You pride yourself upon an animal faculty, in . . . which the negro is your equal and the jackass infinitely your superior!" And there is a proud pathos in his statement, "There *was* a volcano under my ice, but it is burnt out." In his stormy last terms he bitterly denounced the Adams-Clay coalition. His vituperative eccentricity waxed as his sanity waned. He died at fifty-nine in 1833, to the end believing his own epigram: "Asking one of the States to surrender part of her sovereignty is like asking a lady to surrender part of her chastity."

John Randolph, painted by Chester Harding

This daguerreotype of Adams was made shortly before his death. (None of his predecessors in the Presidency had ever posed for a camera.) Adams was stricken in Congress on February 21, 1848, and died two days later. Thomas Hart Benton, his old foe, said, "Where could death have found him but at the post of duty?"

"OLD MAN ELOQUENT"

I adhere to the right of petition," said John Quincy Adams to his fellow congressmen in 1837. "Where," he challenged, "is the degree of vice or immorality which shall deprive the citizen of the right to supplicate for a boon, or to pray for mercy?" Adams, who had feared that he might fall into indolence after his defeat in 1828, was overjoyed at his election to the House two years later. He took on his new job with a rejuvenated independence of mind and spirit. After 1836, when the House passed a gag rule prohibiting the discussion of slavery petitions, Adams devoted much of his energy to fighting the rule. Though opposed to the extension of slavery and hopeful of eventual emancipation, he was not a rabid abolitionist (he decried their "senseless and overbearing clamor"), but he regarded the gag rule as "a direct violation of the Constitution." Annually he badgered the House not to renew it; when ignored, he read antislavery petitions anyway, rushing his words to beat the Speaker's angry gavel. He even read proslavery petitions, including one that asked for his own expulsion from Congress. Often he was hooted at, howled down, threatened with censure. But he persisted, and the gag rule was finally revoked in 1844. Adams' seventeen years in the House of Representatives were his greatest days. Even his adversaries admiringly referred to him as Old Man Eloquent.

CINCINNATI HISTORICAL SOCIETY

Devoted to science, Adams felt astronomy was "one of the most important [subjects] that can engage the attention" of man. In 1843, he gave the address at the cornerstone ceremonies at the observatory on Mount Adams, Ohio (above). Adams also oversaw the creation of the Smithsonian Institution in 1846.

FACTS IN SUMMARY: JOHN QUINCY ADAMS

CHRONOLOGY

UNITED STATES		ADAMS
	1767	*Born July 11*
Declaration of Independence	1776	
Articles of Confederation adopted	1777	
Franco-American alliance	1778	*Sails to France with father*
	1779	*Attends school in Amsterdam*
Articles of Confederation ratified	1781	*Enters Leyden University*
		Travels to St. Petersburg as secretary to American minister
Treaty of Paris	1783	*Resumes studies at The Hague*
		Accompanies father to Paris
	1785	*Returns to U.S.*
Constitutional Convention	1787	*Graduates from Harvard*
Washington elected President	1789	
	1790	*Admitted to the bar*
Jay's Treaty	1794	*Appointed minister to the Netherlands*
John Adams elected President	1796	
	1797	*Marries Louisa Johnson in London*
		Named minister to Prussia

UNITED STATES		ADAMS
Jefferson inaugurated as President	1801	*Returns to U.S.*
	1802	*Elected to Mass. senate*
Louisiana Purchase	1803	*Elected to U.S. Senate*
	1805	*Appointed professor at Harvard*
Madison elected President	1808	*Resigns from Senate*
	1809	*Named minister to Russia*
War with England	1812	
British burn Washington	1814	*Signs Treaty of Ghent*
	1815	*Appointed minister to Great Britain*
Monroe elected President	1816	
	1817	*Named Secretary of State*
	1819	*Negotiates Adams-Onís Treaty annexing Spanish Florida*
Missouri Compromise	1820	
Monroe Doctrine	1823	*Helps draft Monroe's message to Congress*
Democratic-Republicans split into two factions	1825	*Elected President by House of Representatives*
Death of Thomas Jefferson and John Adams	1826	*Nominates delegates to Panama Congress*
Jackson elected President	1828	*Signs "tariff of abominations" into law*
		Ends presidential term

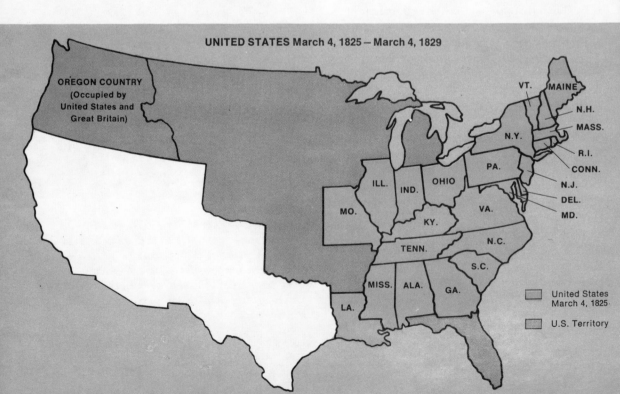

UNITED STATES March 4, 1825 — March 4, 1829

OREGON COUNTRY (Occupied by United States and Great Britain)

VT. MAINE N.H. MASS. N.Y. R.I. CONN. PA. N.J. DEL. MD. ILL. IND. OHIO MO. VA. KY. TENN. N.C. S.C. MISS. ALA. GA. LA.

United States March 4, 1825

U.S. Territory

The "Old House" in Quincy, seen above as it appeared when John Quincy Adams died, was periodically enlarged.

	1830	*Elected to U.S. House of Representatives*
	1831	*Delivers eulogy on James Monroe*
Van Buren elected President	1836	*Opposes extension of slavery*
Tyler assumes Presidency	1841	*Argues Amistad case before Supreme Court*
	1843	*Lays cornerstone of first observatory on Mt. Adams*
Polk elected President	1844	
	1846	*Suffers paralytic stroke*
	1848	*Dies February 23*

BIOGRAPHICAL FACTS

BIRTH: Braintree (Quincy), Mass., July 11, 1767

ANCESTRY: English

FATHER: John Adams; b. Braintree (Quincy), Mass., Oct. 19, 1735; d. Quincy, Mass., July 4, 1826

FATHER'S OCCUPATIONS: Lawyer; statesman; President

MOTHER: Abigail Smith Adams; b. Weymouth, Mass., Nov. 11, 1744; d. Quincy, Mass., Oct. 28, 1818

BROTHERS: Charles (1770–1800); Thomas Boylston (1772–1832)

SISTERS: Abigail Amelia (1765–1813); Susanna (1768–1770)

WIFE: Louisa Catherine Johnson; b. London, England, Feb. 12, 1775; d. Washington, D.C., May 14, 1852

MARRIAGE: London, England, July 26, 1797

CHILDREN: George Washington (1801–1829); John (1803–1834); Charles Francis (1807–1886); Louisa Catherine (1811–1812)

EDUCATION: Studied in Paris, Amsterdam, Leyden, and The Hague; received B.A. (1787) from Harvard; studied law (1788–1790) with Theophilus Parsons

RELIGIOUS AFFILIATION: Unitarian

OCCUPATIONS BEFORE PRESIDENCY: Lawyer; professor

PRE-PRESIDENTIAL OFFICES: Minister to the Netherlands; Minister to Prussia; Member of Mass. Senate; Member of U.S. Senate; Minister to Russia; Minister to Great Britain; Secretary of State

POLITICAL PARTY: Federalist, to 1808; Democratic-Republican, to 1825; National Republican (Whig) thereafter

AGE AT INAUGURATION: 57

OCCUPATIONS AFTER PRESIDENCY: Congressman; writer

DEATH: Washington, D.C., Feb. 23, 1848

PLACE OF BURIAL: First Unitarian Church, Quincy, Mass.

ELECTION OF 1824

(Although Jackson received more votes than Adams, no candidate had a majority, so the election was submitted to the House of Representatives, which chose Adams.)

CANDIDATES	ELECTORAL VOTE	POPULAR VOTE
Andrew Jackson	99	153,544
John Quincy Adams	84	108,740
William H. Crawford	41	46,618
Henry Clay	37	47,136

THE ADAMS ADMINISTRATION

INAUGURATION: March 4, 1825; Hall of the House of Representatives, Washington, D.C.

VICE PRESIDENT: John Calhoun

SECRETARY OF STATE: Henry Clay

SECRETARY OF THE TREASURY: Richard Rush

SECRETARY OF WAR: James Barbour; Peter Buell Porter (from June 21, 1828)

ATTORNEY GENERAL: William Wirt

POSTMASTER GENERAL: John McLean

SECRETARY OF THE NAVY: Samuel Lewis Southard

SUPREME COURT APPOINTMENT: Robert Trimble (1826)

19th CONGRESS (March 4, 1825–March 4, 1827):
Senate: 26 Administration; 20 Jacksonians
House: 105 Administration; 97 Jacksonians

20th CONGRESS (March 4, 1827–March 4, 1829):
Senate: 28 Jacksonians; 20 Administration
House: 119 Jacksonians; 94 Administration

ANDREW JACKSON

I have never seen such a crowd before," said Daniel Webster. "Persons have come five hundred miles to see General Jackson, and they really seem to think that the country has been rescued from some dreadful danger."

The people had come to see "the People's President" inaugurated. They had been descending on Washington for days, by the thousands, filling every inn, sleeping several in a bed, or on billiard tables, or on the floors. Finally the great day arrived: March 4, 1829. It dawned cloudy, but as the vast crowd assembled, the sun broke through and warmed the people who had clogged the streets and were packed onto every terrace, portico, and balcony along Pennsylvania Avenue.

At midmorning the tall, sixty-one-year-old General departed from Gadsby's Tavern, where he had been staying. Some boys perched on nearby window sills caught sight of him and called out excitedly; cannons boomed, and a cheer rose up and resounded down the avenue. As he advanced toward the Capitol, the ailing hero was slowed by the press of the crowd, but he did not seem to mind and he shook every offered hand.

As journalist Anne Royall noted, Andrew Jackson was the most plainly dressed man at the inaugural ceremonies. In deep mourning for his wife, who had died less than three months earlier, the President-elect was attired all in black. He was "thin and pale, and his hair . . . was almost white, and his countenance was melancholy." When he delivered his address, he spoke stiffly and softly, and the pages of the manuscript were seen to tremble in his hand as he turned them. Just as solemn was the Federalist Chief Justice, John Marshall, who must have regarded with extreme distaste the assignment of administering the presidential oath of office to Andrew Jackson.

Andrew Jackson, portrayed in 1833 by Ralph E. W. Earl

As their new President rode horseback to the White House, the crowd followed, sweeping down the avenue, bursting past startled doormen into the Executive Mansion, fighting, scrambling, elbowing, scratching all the while. In the East Room, the mob hurled itself on the refreshments; to the sound of crystal breaking and china smashing, women fainted, fights erupted—noses, clothing, and furniture were bloodied. Presently the riotous assembly—"a regular Saturnalia," one witness called it—became too much for the President to bear. With the help of a wedge of armlocked men, he escaped through a back door and returned to Gadsby's. "The reign of King Mob," observed Supreme Court Justice Joseph Story, "seemed triumphant."

The riot came as no surprise to Jackson's opponents. Throughout the decade preceding the election of 1828, as one state after another eliminated property qualifications for voting, the snowballing power of the common man had placed fear in the hearts of the American upper class. James Kent,

the New York jurist, called attention to the "tendency in the poor to covet a share in the plunder of the rich . . . the industrious and the virtuous; and *there is a tendency in ambitious and wicked men, to inflame these combustible materials.*" Jackson and his supporters were, of course, Kent's ambitious and wicked men. Their campaign to rally the masses behind their cause began in 1824, and casting President John Quincy Adams and his administration in the role of tyrannical oppressors, they captured the Presidency with relative ease in 1828. The rejected political establishment went numb: Secretary of State Henry Clay spent most of the winter at home, lying on his couch under a black cape, as though in mourning; other Cabinet members complained of peculiar diseases; President Adams waited out his term in the White House without a word for his successor and stole away from Washington the night before the inauguration. If any of Jackson's opponents considered the possibility that the people might be something

Among the many gifts Jackson received while in office was a 1,400-pound cheese, four feet in diameter and two feet thick. The People's President offered it to the voters, above, at one of his public receptions.

more than a merciless mob, the disastrous inaugural reception dispelled their doubts. "The country," said John Randolph, "is ruined past redemption."

It was not, of course. But the country had changed. Under the leadership of four Virginia aristocrats and the two Adamses, American farmers, artisans, mechanics, and tradespeople had prospered and blended into a large and ever-growing middle class. By 1828 the nation was theirs, and they declared their ownership official by electing Andrew Jackson to the Presidency. In the spirit of the new America, Jackson changed the office, expanding its scope and power, and reinterpreting its responsibilities.

Andrew Jackson won the people's support for a variety of reasons, but perhaps most significantly because he embodied what was then, and what would remain long after, the American dream. Born poor in a near-wilderness, he had forged success largely on his own, by his strength, his iron will, his exertions and convictions. The people placed him alongside George Washington in their affections—but there was a difference. While Washington was a gentleman-hero, venerated for his devotion to the common cause, Jackson was one of them, a backwoodsman.

Jackson was born in the Waxhaws, a wooded frontier region on the North and South Carolina border, on March 15, 1767. He never knew his father; two weeks before the birth of his third son, the Irish immigrant lifted a heavy log, ruptured something, and died. Andrew's brothers, Hugh and Robert, and an uncle in South Carolina provided him with male companionship and a degree of guidance. He was no scholar, but by the age of five he had been responsive enough to his erratic education to have learned to read, and by eight, to write.

Jackson grew tall and agile, and as a blue-eyed, freckle-faced teen-ager with a thatch of hair as unruly as his hair-trigger temper, he would fight under the least provocation. "Jackson never would give up," recalled one schoolmate, who claimed the ability to "throw him three times out of four," but complained that "he would never *stay* throwed."

When the Revolution came to the Waxhaws in 1780, the Jackson boys joined up. Only Hugh was old enough to be a soldier, and he was killed in battle. Andrew, at thirteen, was a mounted orderly, a carrier of messages, but he did participate in an occasional skirmish. Following one encounter, he and Robert, who was sixteen, were taken prisoner. When Andrew refused a British officer's order to clean his boots, the officer slashed Jackson with a saber, cutting his left arm to the bone and leaving a gash on his head; for good measure, he slashed Robert, too. During a subsequent forty-mile march to a military prison, the Jacksons' wounds were untended, and the boys contracted smallpox. Presently Elizabeth Jackson appeared and persuaded the British commander to release her ailing sons in her custody. Drenched by rain through the long walk home, both boys became delirious. Robert died, but Andrew was saved by his incredible (later legendary) stamina.

Her one surviving son on the mend, Mrs. Jackson set out for Charleston Harbor, where two Jackson cousins lay feverish and in need of nursing aboard a British prison ship. Before long, Andrew received a bundle containing his mother's clothes and a note informing him that she had been buried with other plague victims in an unmarked grave. "I felt utterly alone," Jackson later recalled.

To the people who remembered him, Andrew Jackson emerged from his loneliness "the most roaring, rollicking, game-cocking, horse-racing, card-playing, mischievous fellow . . . the head of rowdies hereabouts. . . ." But Jackson's wildness was not shiftlessness, for he was also extraordinarily ambitious. Not long after his mother's death, he traveled to Salisbury, North Carolina, where he became a law student. In 1788, after completing his studies, he accompanied his friend John McNairy to the Western District of North Carolina (now Tennessee). McNairy had been elected superior court judge for the district, and Jackson went along as public prosecutor.

The Western District was accessible only by an arduous trip through Indian country.

On the Cumberland Road, one hundred and eighty miles beyond civilization, was the settlement of Nashville, where the settlers lived in blockhouses to protect themselves from hostile Indians. It was a developing region, an ideal arena for a young, inexperienced, but eager attorney.

Andrew Jackson moved into the blockhouse of the Widow Donelson, whose daughter, Rachel Robards, had separated from her husband. Rachel's voluptuous beauty attracted the attentions of many men, and Lewis Robards was too jealous to bear having his wife admired. Several months after she left him, however, he arrived at the Donelson house to attempt a reconciliation and was before long suspicious of Andrew Jackson. When Jackson heard about this, he challenged Robards to a duel; the husband refused, and Jackson moved out of the blockhouse. Robards and Rachel eventually returned to Kentucky together, but in 1790, Mrs. Donelson informed Jackson that her daughter again wished to leave her husband. Jackson rode to Kentucky to pick up Rachel and escort her back to the Cumberland Valley. Alleging misconduct between his wife and Jackson, Robards petitioned the Virginia legislature for a bill of divorce. Although the legislature simply gave him permission to take his case to court, Robards allowed the circulation of a rumor that the divorce had taken effect, and in August, 1791, Jackson and Rachel were married.

The divorce would not in fact be effected until two years later, but Jackson was unaware of this and returned to Nashville to resume his career. As a public prosecutor Jackson had been vigorous—in thirty days he had enforced seventy writs of execution—and conservative, generally siding with creditors against debtors. He speculated in land, slaves, and horses, and in that backwoods community he became a man of substance. He satisfied an interest in the military by becoming judge advocate of the county militia, a humble enough beginning for the hero of New Orleans. Skillful with a gun, anti-English and anti-Indian, condescending toward the Tidewater aristocracy, Jackson was, in sum, representative of most border gentlemen.

In December, 1793, Jackson learned that his wife had been legally divorced for only three months. At first he refused to consider remarriage: his pride would not allow him to accept the implication that the first marriage had not been valid; but he was persuaded to reconsider. The second ceremony took place in January, 1794.

In June of 1796, the territory became the state of Tennessee—a name Jackson reputedly gave it—and the rising young attorney was elected, unopposed, to the United States House of Representatives. Albert Gallatin saw him in the House chamber, "a tall, lanky, uncouth-looking personage . . . queue down his back tied with an eel skin . . . manners . . . of a rough backwoodsman." In his one term, Jackson managed to acquire for his state almost twenty-three thousand dollars as compensation for militiamen who had participated in an Indian raid that had taken place against the orders of the federal government. He also distinguished himself by stubbornly refusing to vote for the farewell tribute Congress wanted to tender George Washington. (Jackson disapproved of Jay's Treaty and especially of Washington's gentleness to Indians.) Following his term in the House and a year in the Senate, he resigned his seat to return to Tennessee, for he had been appointed to the superior court of the state. Future reports of his radicalism notwithstanding, the judge was again inclined to be conservative, favoring land barons.

Although Jackson had position and influence, he had not lost his "roaring, rollicking" tendencies, and back in Tennessee, where he was vulnerable to comments regarding his wife and marriage, he had ample opportunity to yield to them. One Saturday morning in October, 1803, on the steps of Jackson's courthouse, Governor John Sevier was elaborating on his own great worth to the state when Jackson stepped forward to recite his contributions. At one point, Sevier sneered, "I know of no great service you have rendered the country, except taking a trip . . . with another man's wife." Jackson instantly

Jackson was commissioned a major general in the United States Army in May of 1814 as a result of successes against the Creek Indians in encounters such as the one at right.

jumped upon Sevier with a howl of rage, clubbing the old soldier with his walking stick. He then challenged Sevier to a duel, but when the two met on the field of honor, they began screaming at each other. Jackson ran at his adversary, threatening to cane him, and Sevier drew his sword, all of which frightened Sevier's horse, which ran away with his pistols. Not a shot was fired.

More serious was Jackson's duel three years later with Charles Dickinson, a dandy who had twice alluded to Rachel's matrimonial record. Jackson took his enemy's shot in the chest, then straightened and aimed. Dickinson, confident of his own aim, staggered back in horror, thinking he had missed; and under the rules (Jackson had not yet fired) he had to return to the mark. Standing with his arms crossed, Dickinson took Jackson's .70-caliber ball in the groin and died a slow, agonizing death. So close was Dickinson's bullet to Jackson's heart that it could not be removed, and Jackson carried it with frequent pain for the rest of his life.

Perhaps Jackson's most famous brawl was one with the Benton brothers, Jesse and Thomas Hart (later a political ally). Tom Benton had criticized Jackson's role as second for a friend in a duel. One day in 1813,

Jackson arrived in Nashville, spotted his critic, and armed with a horsewhip, pursued Benton into a hotel to teach him a lesson. During the melee that followed, Jackson was shot twice. His shoulder was shattered by a bullet, but he refused to have his arm amputated and it was saved.

Jackson's set-to with the Bentons took place during the War of 1812, in which the judge, despite his martial spirit and his credentials (he was then a major general in the United States Volunteers), had participated only briefly. In 1812, Jackson had organized a division and brought it down to Natchez to fight the British, but as soon as he arrived, an order came from Washington to disband —eight hundred miles from home, without supplies or rations. Jackson flatly refused, grumbling about "the wicked machinations" of politicians, and resolved to take the two thousand men home at his own expense. During the difficult journey, one soldier remarked that Jackson was "tough as hickory." Soon the troops were referring to him as Old Hickory.

In 1813, Old Hickory rose from a bed— still bloodstained from the wounds inflicted on him by the Benton brothers—to fight the Creek Indians. The campaign lasted into

1814 and proved to the leaders in Washington that Jackson had tactical skills that could not be ignored. (After his victory, however, Jackson imposed on the Creek a treaty so harsh that the federal government subsequently repudiated much of it. His implacable hostility to Indians was probably his least attractive characteristic.) When the major theater of war shifted south in 1814, the defense of New Orleans fell to him.

First—and without official authorization—Jackson led his men into Spanish Florida and drove the British from Pensacola, which he "liberated" because he felt it should be American (which it soon became). Then he headed for New Orleans, where he tried to block off the six major water routes to the city. Hearing, however, that the British had already taken one, Lake Borgne, and were pressing inland within eight miles of the town, Jackson reportedly sprang up, slapped his hand down on a table, and cried, "By the Eternal, they shall not sleep on our soil!" His counterattack that night is credited by many military historians with having saved the city. Twenty-four hundred British troops had halted their march at the Villeré plantation to await the arrival of reinforcements, another twenty-four hundred men. While they waited, Jackson sent the schooner *Carolina* downstream to shell the British; then he attacked. The following morning, with the enemy thrown off balance by the surprise assault, Jackson retired to defensive positions at the Rodriguez Canal. Then he assembled his men and increased his numbers in preparation for the assault he knew would soon come. To his unit of Kentucky and Tennessee frontiersmen he added regulars and irregulars—Creole dandies, free Negroes, a handful of Choctaw braves, and Jean Lafitte and his pirate crew.

On January 8, 1815, the British regulars—"the conquerors of the conquerors of Europe"—marched into a torrential cross fire. Unable to seize the artillery batteries, which they had planned to turn against the Americans, they found huge chunks blasted from their evenly spaced ranks. The battleground, a flat field with cane stubble, offered no place to hide; the only escape was to the rear. As the front ranks melted away, the following ranks hesitated, then broke. "Never before had British veterans quailed," noted one subaltern sadly, but "that leaden torrent no man on earth could face." After the battle, more than five hundred troopers rose from the heaped mounds of dead comrades to come forward as prisoners. "I never had so grand and awful an idea of the resurrection," said General Jackson. The American casualties: 8 dead, 13 wounded, about 19 missing; the British combined casualties numbered 2,036.

The victory electrified the nation. Ironically, the war was already over (word of peace had not reached Jackson), but the battle gave the young country a needed psychological lift. Andrew Jackson became America's deliverer, its greatest hero since George Washington. At the Place d'Armes in New Orleans, under a triumphal arch, a little girl sang to the General while dozens of others strewed flower petals in his path.

After the war, Andrew Jackson solidified his new national eminence by keeping active in the Florida area, where expansionist eyes had logically turned. The Spanish had had much difficulty controlling East Florida, locale of considerable privateering with many rebels claiming to represent an assortment of governments. Aided by unauthorized British soldiers, Seminole and Creek raided the Georgia border; American troops arrived and chased the Indians deeper into Florida, and American settlers promptly moved in. As the Indians retaliated, President Monroe sent Jackson to lead troops against them but instructed him not to attack those who retreated into Spanish forts. Jackson, however, anxious to take "the whole of East Florida," seized the town of St. Marks in 1818, which he claimed was under Indian attack. He then marched to a Seminole village and burned it down; then he accused two British subjects of aiding the Indians and executed them. In May, he advanced on Pensacola and deposed the Spanish governor, installing in his place one of his own officers. President Monroe

Jean François Vallée, obviously influenced by portraits of Napoleon, made a miniature of General Jackson, right, at New Orleans in 1815. Edward Livingston, to whom Jackson presented the painting with the inscription above, had the confidence of many of the region's key figures; he roused support for Jackson and helped plan the city's defense.

denied ever giving Jackson permission to enter the Spanish colony, but there is a letter from Secretary of War Calhoun to the governor of Alabama which says that Jackson had been "vested with full power to conduct the war as he may think best." In any case, despite the misgivings of some in the Capital, Jackson's activities were widely championed in rural America. In 1821, Monroe appointed him governor of Florida, which had been officially ceded by Spain in 1819. Jackson served only four months and then returned to Nashville, where he was called on by a steady stream of politicians and men of public affairs. They wanted him to be President of the United States.

Jackson was not immediately amenable to the idea. "Do they think," he asked, "that I am such a damned fool as to think myself fit for President of the United States? No, sir; I know what I am fit for. I can command a body of men in a rough way; but I am not fit to be President." Within a year, however, the idea began to take hold of him. It was not unusual in 1822 to see newspaper items similar to the one in the Nashville *Whig* of July 17: "GREAT RACING!! . . . The prize to be run for is the *Presidential Chair*. . . . There have already four states sent their nags in. Why not Tennessee put in her stud? and if so, let it be called *Old Hickory*. . . ."

There were at least two good reasons why he should not make the attempt. First,

Rachel would have preferred that he did not. Each of her husband's public services left her bereaved, anxiously awaiting his return. And second, Jackson's health was in a perilous state. "He is not a well man and never will be unless they allow him to rest," wrote Rachel to her niece. "In the thirty years of our wedded life . . . he has not spent one-fourth of his days under his own roof. . . ." But Jackson's ability to ignore the frailty of his body and to overcome his various infirmities was nothing short of incredible: during the Creek campaign he came down with severe dysentery, from which he never fully recovered. In 1821, he wrote to a friend that in addition to a chronic cough and lung inflammation, "I have been recently vissitted by my old bowwel complaint, which has weakened me very much . . . in short Sir I must take rest or my stay here on Earth cannot be long. . . ." By 1822, however, the General was clearly reconciled to the role of undeclared candidate. Taking advice from Senator John Henry Eaton of Tennessee, he refused Monroe's offer of a ministerial appointment, but, against his wishes, he was elected senator and went to Washington.

The year 1824 was one of transition in the United States. Property qualifications for voting were eliminated in some states but retained in others; electors were chosen here by state legislators, there by districts, elsewhere by blocks. All the candidates were

213

Jeffersonian Republicans. John Quincy Adams was expected to take the urban Northeast and share the old Federalist vote with William H. Crawford, who would be strong in the South. The new popular vote and Western vote were sought by Henry Clay and Andrew Jackson. The final count on election day was Jackson 99, Adams 84, Crawford 41, and Clay 37. In the absence of a majority, the election was thrown to the House, where after weeks of intrigue, Clay threw his support to Adams, and Adams won. Jackson resigned his Senate seat and immediately began the campaign to win in 1828. Sabotaging Adams' programs whenever they could, his supporters kept the President under an unfriendly spotlight for four years.

As the election date neared, the campaign became low beyond all tradition. Colonel Charles Hammond, editor of the Cincinnati *Gazette* and a crony of Henry Clay's, asked in a pamphlet, "Ought a convicted adultress and her paramour husband to be placed in the highest offices of this free and christian land?" As a presidential candidate, Jackson could not demand a duel but he fervently vowed that "a day of retribution . . . [for] Mr. Clay and his tool Colonel Hammond must arrive. . . ." *The Coffin Handbill* was a widely circulated pamphlet detailing through words and pictures the deaths of John Woods (a mutineer Jackson had executed during the Creek War) and six Tennessee militiamen executed in Alabama. The handbill also showed Jackson sticking a sword into the neck of someone who had stopped to pick up something from the street. Nevertheless, the Adams-Clay forces were on the defensive; the common man was in charge now, and he wanted Jackson, who won by an electoral vote of 178 to 83.

Perhaps the most pathetic victim of the campaign was Rachel Jackson. A visitor found her "once a form of rotund and rubiscund beauty . . . now very plethoric and obese. . . . [She] talked low but quick, with a short and wheezing breath." On December 17, 1828, she suffered an apparent heart attack and a few days later developed symp-

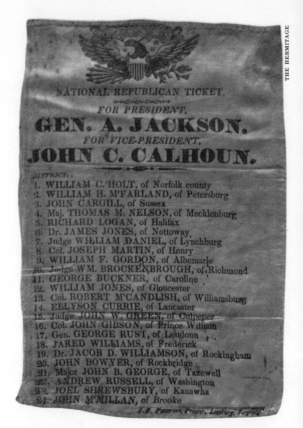

Ambitious John Calhoun of South Carolina settled for second spot on the Jackson ticket, above.

toms of pleurisy. On the night of the twenty-second she told her maid that she would "rather be a door-keeper in the house of God than to live in that palace [the White House]." Twenty minutes later, General Jackson, in the adjoining room, heard her say, "I am fainting." He rushed to her, lifted her to the bed, and felt the convulsion of her muscles as her life ended. At the funeral Jackson wept bitterly. He spoke of "those vile wretches" who had destroyed his "dear saint." Out loud he cried, "May God Almighty forgive her murderers, as I know she forgave them. I never can."

The next month the President-elect set out for Washington. Along the route the people came out to see him, but they were quiet, respecting his grief. On the boat from Cincinnati to Washington, according to a contemporary account, "a greasy fellow" said to him, "'General Jackson, I guess?'

The General bowed assent. 'Why they told me you was dead.' 'No! Providence has hitherto preserved my life.' 'And is your wife alive, too?' The General, apparently much hurt, signified the contrary, upon which the man concluded by saying, 'Ay, I thought it was the one or the t'other of ye.' "

So Andrew Jackson arrived in Washington, and the American republic became the Jacksonian democracy, where an ambitious, young, and vigorous people placed all their trust in an aging, ill, and mournful man who was, they thought, a symbol of themselves. To the factions he had defeated, Old Hickory was a radical; yet in political service he had tended to be conservative. In truth, no one knew what sort of President Andrew Jackson would be. "My opinion is," wrote Daniel Webster, "that when he comes he will bring a breeze with him. Which way it will blow, I cannot tell. . . ." Senator William Marcy of New York once commented that the politicians of his state "see nothing wrong in the rule that to the VICTOR belong the spoils of the ENEMY." Rotation in office was nothing new—Thomas Jefferson had removed 10 per cent of the officials in John Adams' administration when he took office—but the phrase "spoils system" had a dirty ring to it. When during his first eighteen months in office Jackson replaced about the same percentage of appointees, his opponents contended that he had "introduced corruption into the central government. . . ." The President never denied employing the system; he did deny that it was corrupt. Rotation in office, he explained, broke up an entrenched bureaucracy and prevented government from becoming a continuous "engine for the support of the few at the expense of the many."

Jackson's first major crisis in the White House was not outwardly a political matter, although it did have great political repercussions. Margaret O'Neale, daughter of a tavern keeper who was a friend of Jackson's and Senator John Eaton's, was a dark-haired, round-faced vamp, pampered, self-centered, and vivacious. Before she was sixteen, she had to her credit one suicide, one duel, one

nearly ruined and greatly damaged military career, and one aborted elopement. Then, at sixteen, she married a landlocked Navy purser, John B. Timberlake. Presently, Eaton, infatuated with Peggy, had Timberlake sent to sea and kept there, and sought out the young bride in order to console her. The plan apparently worked, and Washington society watched with great concern the scandalous developments of the affair. The First Lady, Mrs. James Monroe, ostracized the couple, and the other ladies of the Capital followed suit. In 1828, Timberlake died at sea from disease or drink, although Washington preferred to believe that Timberlake had cut his throat because of his wife's unfaithfulness. President-elect Jackson, who was either terribly naïve, terribly realistic, or just plain sympathetic—he was certainly sensitive to the problems of a woman's reputation—told Eaton, whom he intended to name Secretary of War, that he must marry Peggy Timberlake to "shut their mouths." The couple married on January 1, 1829.

Jackson's Cabinet was divided down the middle by the affair. Vice President John C. Calhoun, a brilliant, arrogant gentleman who wanted to be tapped for the presidential succession, could not (and apparently did not try to) bring his wife and the wives of other Cabinet members into line. They continued to ostracize Mrs. Eaton. On the other hand, Secretary of State Martin Van Buren, a widower with presidential aspirations of his own, remained perfectly courteous to the Eatons. Calhoun hoped that by embarrassing Eaton he would force the Secretary to resign, thus weakening the influence of Van Buren. But Eaton would not resign, nor would the President ask him to. Until April, 1831, the Eaton affair continued to divide the administration and interfere with the business of government; then, suddenly and simply, Van Buren, the "Little Magician," produced a magic cure: he resigned. When Eaton took the hint and resigned, too, Jackson was able to ask the rest of the Cabinet—the Calhoun wing—for resignations. It was as though a great weight had fallen from the General's shoulders.

215

The statuette above of King Louis Philippe and Jackson is carved from hickory and commemorates the payment of a French indemnity to the United States.

Jackson's Cabinet was rebuilt, and Van Buren sailed for London as minister to the Court of St. James's to wait for his reward in 1832. Calhoun and the President fell further apart, a process accelerated by Jackson's discovery that the Vice President had, contrary to his claims, spoken against the General's Florida adventure in 1818, and by Calhoun's success at getting the Senate to deny confirmation of Van Buren's London appointment. Amos Kendall, a frontier editor who had once been pro-Clay, became fourth auditor of the Treasury and chief adviser in Jackson's "Kitchen Cabinet." Now that he had his own men around him and the intra-administration problems were behind him, Jackson was ready to enforce his program.

He felt that the Chief Executive was responsible for the protection of "the liberties and rights of the people and the integrity of the Constitution against the Senate, or the House of Representatives, or both together." And to make certain that the few never gained at the expense of the many—the measurement he generally used before taking a stand on an issue—he was prepared to use all the muscle at the disposal of the Presidency. He had already indicated that he would not hesitate to employ a veto. In 1830, Jackson had vetoed the Maysville Road bill, which committed government funds to the construction of roads entirely within the state of Kentucky, on the grounds that it benefited too small a percentage of those who would have to pay for it. Jackson thus came out against the internal improvements plank of Henry Clay's "American System." He would use the veto more frequently than any prior President, and Clay would deplore the "concentration of all power in the hands of one man."

Jackson also took aim at another keystone of the American System—the Bank of the United States. In his first annual message to Congress, the President voiced doubts about both the constitutionality and expediency of the Bank. No action was then necessary, however, because the Bank charter was not due to expire until 1836. But, as early as 1831, Jackson told Charles Carroll, last surviving signer of the Declaration of Independence, that he intended to stand for re-election "upon the principle of putting the bank down. . . . No bank and Jackson— or bank and no Jackson." His hostility reflected his suspicion of paper money and his conviction that the Bank created an alliance between business and government and resulted in benefits to the few at cost to many. The president of the Bank, Nicholas Biddle, tried in 1830 and 1831 to woo Jackson, but when his efforts proved fruitless, he agreed to have Clay and Webster make the Bank the major issue of the election of 1832.

In June the recharter passed the Senate. In July it passed the House. That evening, while a nightlong victory celebration rocked Biddle's lodgings, Jackson looked over the recharter bill with Van Buren, who had just returned from England to be Jackson's vice presidential candidate. "The bank, Mr. Van

Buren," said the President, "is trying to kill me." Then he matter-of-factly added, *"but I will kill it!"*

A week later, on July 10, Jackson sent his veto message to Congress: "It is to be regretted that the rich and powerful too often bend the acts of government to their selfish purposes. . . . Distinctions in society will always exist under every just government . . . but when the laws undertake to add to these natural and just advantages artificial distinctions . . . to make the rich richer and the potent more powerful, the humble members of society—the farmers, mechanics, and laborers—who have neither the time nor the means of securing like favors to themselves, have a right to complain of the injustice of their Government." The veto held, despite Biddle's cries of outrage.

Although the Bank was not rechartered, it was not yet dead, but before issuing his final thrust Jackson had other matters to deal with. South Carolina had been giving Jackson trouble since the start of his administration. The tariff of 1828, known as the "tariff of abominations," was the object

of much animosity in the South because the protection of Northern manufacturing necessarily produced a loss in the South of overseas trade. John Calhoun wrote the *South Carolina Exposition*, which included the "Protest Against the Tariff of 1828 and the principles of Nullification." When another, equally oppressive, tariff was passed in 1832, the state legislature adopted the Ordinance of Nullification, which declared the tariff void, not "binding upon this State, its officers or citizens."

Jackson had clashed with Calhoun over the issue before, at a dinner honoring Thomas Jefferson on April 13, 1830. Following twenty-four carefully prepared toasts, mostly in support of South Carolina, the President rose and waited out the cheers. Van Buren was so excited he climbed onto his chair to watch. Jackson fixed his attention on Calhoun and paused to savor the drama of the moment. Finally he raised his glass: "Our Union: It must be preserved." In the charged atmosphere, all rose to drink, including Calhoun, clearly shaken to the core. The Vice President's hand trembled; wine trickled down the side of his glass. When order was restored and he was called on for a toast, Calhoun stuck to his guns: "The Union, next to our liberty, most dear."

South Carolina's Ordinance of Nullification and threats of secession were a clear challenge to federal authority. Jackson acted swiftly. "No state or states has a right to secede . . ." he said. "Nullification therefore means insurrection and war; and other states have a right to put it down." But in his annual message, on December 4, 1832, he was more conciliatory, proposing a lowered tariff as a compromise. John Quincy Adams, who had returned to Washington as a congressman, believed this to be "a complete surrender to the nullifiers." But before the week was out, he issued a proclamation to the people of South Carolina, a statement strong enough even for Adams, Webster, and

PLAIN SEWING DONE HERE

SYMPTOMS OF A LOCKED JAW

Henry Clay was successful—as the cartoon on the left clearly indicates—in quashing Jackson's protest against Senate censure of his anti-Bank policies.

217

Emily Donelson, the President's young niece and hostess, sat for the portrait above in 1830. She snubbed Peggy Eaton, much to Jackson's displeasure.

the other staunch Unionists: "Disunion by armed force is *treason*. Are you ready to incur its guilt?" Then he had a bill introduced in the Senate that would authorize the President to use force to sustain federal authority. Jackson was prepared to send an army to South Carolina, but his will proved stronger than the pride of the nullifiers. A token compromise tariff was passed, which enabled the state to rescind its ordinance.

The Union had been preserved, and Jackson's popularity was soaring. He and Van Buren had overwhelmingly won the 1832 election, and the next spring, Jackson set out on a triumphal tour. In Baltimore, Philadelphia, New York, even in New England, where he had gained prestige through his vigorous defense of the Union and his new cordial relations with Daniel Webster, the old General was received with tumultuous welcomes.

Because of his failing health and developments in his war against the Bank of the United States, Jackson cut his tour short and returned to the Capital. The Bank char-

ter was about to expire, and the President's veto of the recharter had not been overridden. His more conservative advisers, Van Buren among them, suggested that Jackson had done enough; but the more radical, led by Kendall, thought that the government should remove its funds from the Bank, for otherwise the unchartered Bank would remain solvent. That being the case, a Congress fearful for the future of its deposits might well reconsider and vote for recharter after all. After first removing Secretary of the Treasury William J. Duane and replacing him with Roger B. Taney, who supported removal of public funds, Jackson dictated that after October 1, 1833, no federal deposits were to be made, and issued the first call for removal of funds.

Nicholas Biddle fought back ferociously. "All the other Banks and all the merchants may break," he wrote to a friend, "but the Bank of the United States shall not break." Biddle had given the nation its strongest currency, and he was not about to see his accomplishments undone. Tightening credit, calling in loans, reducing discounts, he meant to demonstrate the power of the Bank by creating a panic—and he succeeded. Some of those ruined were the Bank's most vigorous supporters. Finally, in 1834, Biddle succumbed to the pressure and eased up on his restrictive policies, unwittingly proving that his ruinous measures had not been necessary in the first place. Ironically, the Bank was enjoying a period of expansion when the charter expired in 1836. Rechartered as a state bank in Pennsylvania it eventually failed, and countless depositors were ruined.

The President's victory was a mixed blessing. The public deposits that had been transferred to state banks—Jackson's "pet banks," the opposition called them—and the loosening of credit led to an increased production of paper money. As a result of the inflation that followed, Jackson issued his "Specie Circular" of July 11, 1836, which stated that thenceforth the government would accept only specie, gold or silver, in land payments. As a result, inflation was curbed, but a depression struck in 1837 nonetheless.

During his last days in the White House, Jackson was concerned with an international matter: since 1821, American slaveowners had been settling in Texas. When Mexico won its independence, its government declared Texas a state but left it open for colonization. On April 8, 1830, however, the Mexicans passed a law forbidding slavery and the further colonization of Texas by Americans. Throughout the following five years, the American settlers took steps to separate from Mexico, and in 1835, Santa Anna abolished all local rights in the state and took an army of six thousand across the Rio Grande to deal with the insurrectionists. While the dictator-soldier was defeating the rebels at the Alamo, a convention declared Texan independence on March 2, 1836. Seven weeks later, Sam Houston reversed the trend and whipped the Mexicans at San Jacinto.

Congress passed resolutions calling for recognition of Texas early in July, but the President hesitated. The United States had recognized the Mexican republic, and Jackson felt that he was obliged to honor that government's sovereignty in what was technically an internal struggle. Moreover, the Whigs opposed recognition on the grounds that it was a Southern trick to broaden slavery. Personally, Jackson owned slaves and saw nothing wrong with the institution, but 1836 was an election year; his hand-picked successor, Martin Van Buren, was a candidate, and he did not wish to hurt his chances in the North by allowing the slavery issue to creep into the campaign. On March 3, 1837, however, with Van Buren safely elected, the President appointed an American representative to Houston's government, thereby effecting recognition of the new republic.

TEXAS STATE ARCHIVES

Texas insurgents took Fort San Antonio de Bexar (above) in 1835, but early the following March some three thousand Mexicans regained the town after besieging a 187-man force at the Alamo for thirteen days.

The next day the Presidency of Andrew Jackson ended. In eight years he had thoroughly altered the course of American government. His mistakes had been many, his prejudices legion, his actions guided less by law than by ego and instincts; yet his impact on the office has been matched by few.

Jackson represented a complete break from his sophisticated, intellectual predecessors. While their paternalistic attitude toward the common man may have been outdated, their concern for the people was in many ways greater than Jackson's. Thomas Jefferson and John Quincy Adams wanted all Americans to have education in advance of suffrage; Jackson was content to take advantage of the broad suffrage and was in no rush to educate the people. The first six Presidents wanted slavery abolished; most made at least token attempts to treat the Indians fairly. Jackson was for equality for all white men.

Jackson often referred to the law to justify his actions, but his positions were really assumed on the basis of how Jackson felt about them. His stated opposition to the Bank of the United States was spotted with references to constitutionality, yet an 1819 Supreme Court decision had declared the Bank perfectly constitutional. The almost sanctified concept of "Union" was enough to justify his firmness with regard to South Carolina's Ordinance of Nullification; but because he had no liking for Indians, Jackson did nothing when Georgia nullified a federal treaty. On Georgia lands guaranteed by the United States, the Cherokee Indians were laboring to develop a civilized society based on their own folkways but updated to be compatible with American society. They had renounced war, had cooperated with whites, and were well on their way to establishing a system of self-government when Georgia, claiming the right to overrule federal law, ordered the Cherokee off the land. The Indians remained committed to the rule of law. Instead of raising arms they took their case to the Supreme Court—and won. Again insisting it had the right to nullify the rule of any federal branch, Georgia proceeded to ex-pel the Cherokee. This was in 1832, at the same time that Jackson was telling South Carolina that nullification was "treason."

Yet Jackson is considered a great President. The first popularly elected Chief Executive, he pitted himself against the congressmen and senators who served some, while he acted for all. What Jackson grasped was not necessarily the essential fiber of an issue but the way people felt about it. Thus, his wisdom was the wisdom of the masses, his accomplishments the people's. As Clinton Rossiter wrote, "more than one such President a century would be hard to take. Yet he was a giant in his influence on our system . . . and second only to Washington in terms of influence on the Presidency."

Jackson was seventy when he retired to "The Hermitage," his home in Tennessee. Unfortunately, the monumental inability of his adopted son, Andrew, Jr., to hold on to a dollar made his retirement less leisurely than the General might have liked, and he had to spend much of his time going over books and trying to raise funds. He retained an interest and considerable power in his party—enough to dictate the nomination of the dark horse Polk, his protégé, for the Presidency in 1844.

He wrote to Polk on June 6, 1845, revealing that his mind was still vigorous; but according to historian J. W. Ward, "his flesh from the waist down had literally to be wrapped to his body to keep it from falling away." On June 8, he fainted, and a spoonful of brandy was administered to revive him. Late in the afternoon Andrew, Jr., asked the General if he knew him. Jackson said he did and asked for his spectacles. Shortly thereafter he died.

The Jacksonian Era continued, however. In the years between the election of Old Hickory and the election of Lincoln the only way the opposition could loosen the Jacksonian hold on the Presidency was by nominating two old soldiers who reminded the people of Jackson. Lincoln ended the Jacksonian Era. But even he would use the Jacksonian concept of the Presidency to fashion his own power and preserve the Union.

—SAUL BRAUN

Andrew Jackson

A PICTURE PORTFOLIO

*The life-sized cast-iron bullfrog seen above is one
of the most unique items from Jackson's campaigns.*

GAVEL AND SWORD

In 1787, twenty-year-old Andrew Jackson was well equipped to make a name for himself in North Carolina's Western District. An arduous childhood had left him tall, straight, and spare with a thin, fair face and arresting blue eyes. A fine horseman and superior marksman, he was athletic, intelligent, ambitious—and already a licensed lawyer. In the next dozen years he served as district attorney, helped draw up the constitution when the District became Tennessee, sat in Congress in Washington, and was elected to the state superior court. Jackson bought The Hermitage and seemed

When a British officer, above, slashed his insubordinate prisoner, Andy Jackson, with his saber in 1781, he left the youth with a permanent scar on his hand and an equally permanent antipathy toward the English.

to aspire only to the life of a country gentleman. But he was elected major general of the state militia in 1802; when he resigned his judgeship in 1804 to retire to private life, he retained his military commission. It would be the sword, not the gavel, that would ultimately lead him to the Presidency.

The miniature above of Jackson in Army uniform was painted on ivory by Anna Claypoole Peale.

The certificate below, issued in 1796, permitted Jackson to practice law in the new state of Tennessee. The document was signed by Governor John Sevier, who became Jackson's bitter enemy.

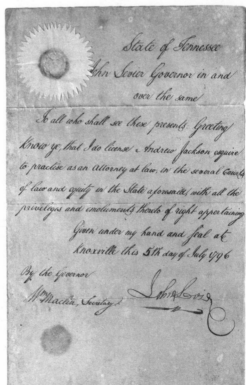

VICTORY
AT NEW ORLEANS

I will smash them, so help me God!" thundered Andrew Jackson upon hearing that an advance British force was nearing New Orleans. The engagement that evening, December 23, 1814, was indecisive, but it forestalled the British build-up for two weeks. Jackson's men had time to create and fortify an earthen embankment along a canal traversing the only route the enemy could take to New Orleans. On the morning of January 8, 1815, a heavy fog lifted and Jackson saw some 5,300 well-drilled redcoats marching directly toward the embankment. Three waves of Britons were raked by artillery and devastating rifle fire from rows of Jackson's sharpshooters. Only one Englishman gained the rampart unhurt; he looked behind him and discovered that his men "had vanished as if the earth had swallowed them up." More than two thousand British were killed or wounded that day, while American casualties totaled about forty. It was an overwhelming victory for General Jackson, who learned two months after the battle that a peace treaty between England and the United States had been signed in Europe in December.

The medal above was authorized by a joint congressional resolution on February 27, 1815. The resolution lauded Jackson and his motley troops for "uniform gallantry and good conduct" on January 8, when they won "a most signal victory . . . with a disparity of loss . . . unexampled in military annals."

At the center of the painting below, Major General Sir Edward Pakenham, commander of the British forces at New Orleans, lies dying from a charge of grapeshot. Historian Marquis James likened the redcoats, falling from their ranks under the murderous gunfire, to "teeth snapping from a comb."

NEW ORLEANS

GENERAL PACKENHAM

January 1815.

Generall Jackson and his Lady

Andrew and Rachel Jackson celebrate his great victory at New Orleans in the painting at left by a contemporary folk artist.

THE HERMITAGE

Jackson always kept with him the miniature of Rachel, above, by Anna C. Peale.

"I HAVE NEVER WISHED IT"

Slander and separation beset Rachel Donelson Jackson throughout her adult life; in 1828, they killed her. The slander arose from her mismarriage to Lewis Robards, and her subsequent, invalid first wedding to Andrew Jackson. The resultant calumny was an enduring source of sorrow to her and a forge of bitterness, anger, and frustration for Jackson. Rachel loved her husband with absolute devotion, but the trauma of her first marriage understandably abetted her wish to share with him a quiet life of simple, private pleasures at The Hermitage. As Jackson rose in the uncertain realms of politics and the military, Rachel's dreams of that life were only intermittently realized. ". . . you have served your Country Long Enough . . ." she wrote the General in 1814, "you have been gon six monthes. . . . oh Lord of heaven how Can I beare it." Since the early 1790's Rachel had been alone often, as her husband had pursued his legal career as a means to money and reputation. When he sat in Congress in 1796, he left her behind. Friends crowded The Hermitage when Jackson was elected to the state superior court in 1798, but Rachel was shy of them. She often spoke of Andrew as "Mr. Jackson," never "Judge," seldom "General."

Florida claimed much of Jackson's time after the War of 1812, and Rachel regretted his acceptance of its governorship. But when he resigned in October of 1821 she was happy at the prospect of returning to The Hermitage for, as Jackson put it, the "ballance of our lives." But her apprehensions soon were rekindled: in 1822 she wrote, "They talk of his being President. . . . But I hope he may not be called again to the strife and empty honors of public place." And when he was called, in 1828, she said, "For Mr. Jackson's sake I am glad. For my own part I have never wished it." Small wonder—for in that election campaign her name had been dragged through the mud again and again, and candidate Jackson could not settle matters with a pistol as citizen Jackson had done in earlier years. In late December of 1828, the years of casual gossip and outright slander, and of anxiety for her adored husband, took their toll on Rachel. Over the grave of his "dear saint," the grief-stricken President-elect warned that "those vile wretches who have slandered her must look to God for mercy."

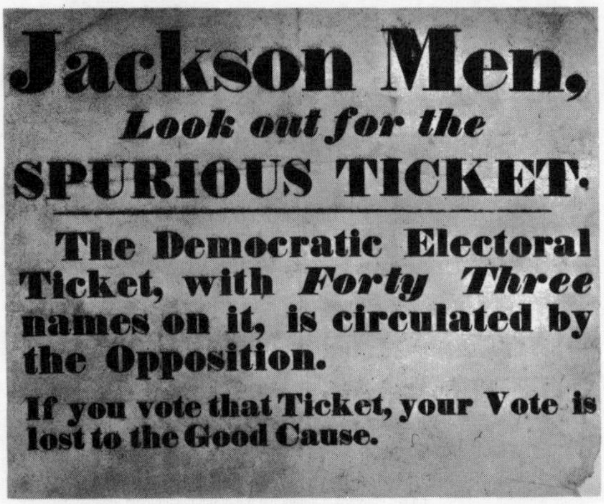

Jackson Men,
Look out for the
SPURIOUS TICKET.

The Democratic Electoral Ticket, with *Forty Three* names on it, is circulated by the Opposition.

If you vote that Ticket, your Vote is lost to the Good Cause.

The poster above is indicative of the deviousness to which the 1828 campaigning descended. In the pell-mell rush to assassinate Jackson's character, administration forces sometimes acted rashly. Jackson's early dealings with Aaron Burr were deplored—until it was recalled that Secretary of State Henry Clay had been a defense attorney for one of Burr's associates.

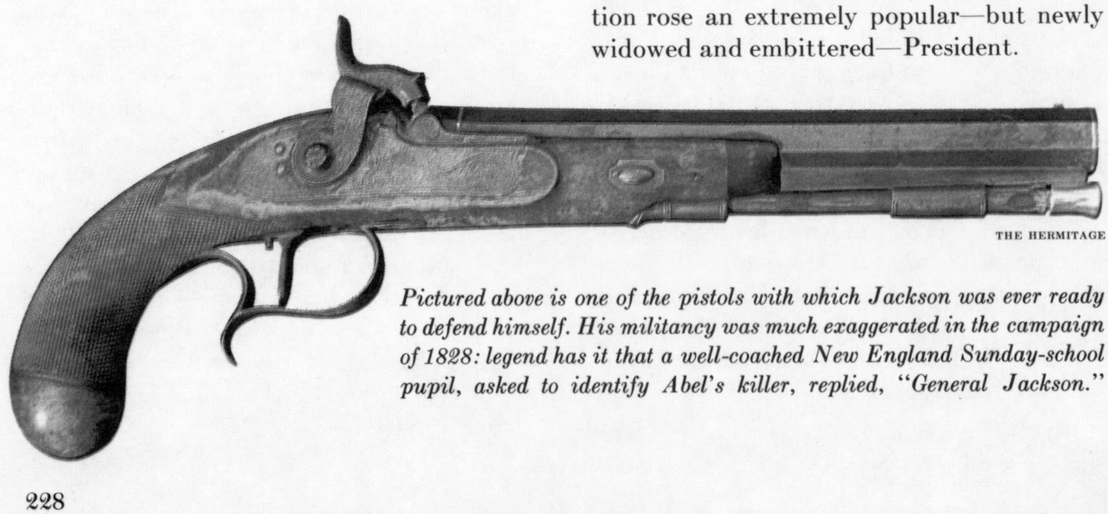

A FOUL CAMPAIGN

All that is necessary for you is to be still and quiet," advised Senator John Eaton in 1826. "Say nothing and plant cotton." Presidential aspirant Andrew Jackson did pretty much just that: he was enjoying a prolonged residence at The Hermitage for the first time in years. The excitement over the "corrupt bargain" between Henry Clay and President John Quincy Adams was clearly working against the administration. In Washington, a corps of counselors labored effectively on Jackson's behalf. The only real issues of the day, the tariff and internal improvements, found Jackson and Adams in substantial accord; it seemed certain that the election of 1828 would be decided on the basis of the candidates' personalities, and the 1824 campaign had proven that Jackson was more popular than Adams. But late in 1826, the slander against Rachel Jackson began in earnest, and the campaign became one of the most putrid in American history; Jackson himself was called the son of a prostitute and a mulatto. The Jackson press, to the disgust of its candidate, countered with allegations of premarital impropriety between President and Mrs. Adams. From the mire of the election rose an extremely popular—but newly widowed and embittered—President.

THE HERMITAGE

Pictured above is one of the pistols with which Jackson was ever ready to defend himself. His militancy was much exaggerated in the campaign of 1828: legend has it that a well-coached New England Sunday-school pupil, asked to identify Abel's killer, replied, "General Jackson."

228

Some Account of some of the Bloody Deeds of
GEN. JACKSON.

Jacob Webb.   David Morrow.   John Harris.   Henry Lewis.   David Hunt.   Edward Lindsey.

The Coffin Handbill, *above, condemned Jackson as a bloodthirsty disciplinarian for ordering the execution of six mutinous militiamen in 1815. The broadside was circulated during the campaign of 1828.*

"*Jackson is to be President, and you will be HANGED.*"

The hanged man is unidentified, but it is clear that presidential nominee Jackson is the executioner.

Peggy Eaton (shown at right, in a daguerreotype made long after the political storm she caused was over) was said to have lived with Secretary of War John Eaton before their marriage, and to have given birth to two of Eaton's children while she was still Mrs. John Timberlake. Jackson, who recalled only too well the slander directed against his own wife, was infuriated by the malicious gossip. He called a special Cabinet meeting (depicted below; Peggy did not attend the actual conference, however) to discuss the matter. Finding no "complete establishment" of a case against her, Andrew Jackson thought Peggy vindicated. But the defamation campaign, led by John Calhoun's wife, Floride, continued unabated until the Jackson Cabinet was reorganized in 1831.

THE EATON AFFAIR

If you love Margaret Timberlake," said President-elect Jackson to his old friend Senator John Eaton in 1828, "go and marry her . . . forthwith." Eaton did as he was told, but Washington gossips remained convinced that the pretty widow had a long history of promiscuity. Peggy Timberlake Eaton was summarily snubbed by the town's elite, but as the time for naming a Cabinet drew near (Eaton was to be Jackson's Secretary of War), the slander campaign eased, only to be redoubled after the inauguration. The sniping soon resulted in a full-scale political war of nerves: the President stoutly defended Eaton and his wife ("She is as chaste as a virgin!"), and Secretary of State Van Buren supported him. Vice President Calhoun, vying with Van Buren to succeed Jackson, was in opposition—were Eaton to fall, and drag Van Buren with him, Calhoun would have clear sailing. "Calhoun leads the moral party," was John Quincy Adams' wry comment, "Van Buren that of the frail sisterhood." Cannily, Van Buren resigned in 1831, permitting a reorganization of the Cabinet. Van Buren was clearly in line for the Vice Presidency, and Calhoun had yet another wound to lick.

"King Andrew the First," as Jackson's detractors called him, is depicted in a cartoon of 1832, above, as a veto-wielding tyrant who has trampled on the Constitution, the Supreme Court, and the National Bank.

231

"THE SOUTH,
THE POOR SOUTH"

If one drop of blood be shed [in South Carolina] in defiance of the laws of the United States," growled Andrew Jackson in 1832, "I will hang the first man of [the Nullifiers] I can get my hands on. . . ." Such drastic measures were never necessary, but Jackson always regretted not being able to hang John Caldwell Calhoun, the very voice of nullification.

In 1810, at the beginning of his congressional career, Calhoun was an ardent nationalist. Declaring that "Our true system is to look to the country . . . to advance the general interest," he supported the War of 1812, internal improvements, a national bank, and protective tariffs. After seven years as Monroe's Secretary of State, he joined the 1824 presidential free-for-all and won the Vice Presidency under John Quincy Adams. But Calhoun sensed the imminent swing to Jackson, and as Senate president, permitted antiadministration oratory from Adams' detractors. ("Calhoun veers round in his politics . . ." Adams charged, "and makes his intellect pander to his will.") He was rewarded by being re-elected to the Vice Presidency under Jackson, whom he hoped to succeed. But Calhoun's animosity toward Peggy Eaton and his attempts to discredit Van Buren rankled Jackson, who was also furious when he discovered that Calhoun had criticized his conduct during the Florida campaign of 1818. But it was Calhoun's espousal of nullification that made the break with Jackson final.

In earlier years, Calhoun had been reprimanded by the Southern press for failing to abandon his protectionist stance. By 1827, however, he had come to believe that high tariffs and growing antislavery sentiment posed dire threats to the Southern economy.

His *South Carolina Exposition*, published anonymously in 1828, presented the theory that any state could annul a federal law it disapproved. Hopes that Jackson would support this states' rights principle were dashed at a Jefferson Day dinner in 1830, when Jackson, staring directly at Calhoun, made his famous toast: "Our Union: It must be preserved."

The Nullification Crisis reached its boiling point in 1832, when South Carolina proclaimed federal tariffs not "binding upon this State." When Jackson issued a proclamation stating that nullification could not be abided, Calhoun resigned the Vice Presidency, was appointed senator from South Carolina, and, amid saber rattling on both sides, led the fight in the Senate. A compromise tariff averted violence, but Calhoun's course was irrevocably plotted. In the Senate, as Secretary of State under Tyler, and in his writings, he feverishly deplored abolition and outlined his theory of "concurrent majorities." Rule by a numerical majority, he held, was "but Government of the strongest interests," which, "when not efficiently checked, is the most tyrannical and oppressive that can be devised. . . ." He stated flatly that "the will of a majority is the will of a rabble. Progressive democracy is incompatible with liberty." Out-of-power interests, namely the South, should be given the "right of self-protection": each state should have, he said, the power to concur in or veto any federal legislation.

"If trampled upon," he warned the nation in 1847, "it will be idle to expect that we will not resist." Frustration, failing health, and his own humorless intensity ground Calhoun down. He died in 1850, lamenting to the end the fate of "the South, the poor South."

The polar changes in the political philosophy of John Calhoun were mirrored in his physiognomy, as the illustrations on the left so strikingly indicate. The portrait, top, a copy of a painting by Charles B. King, shows him in his nationalist period when he was, said John Quincy Adams, "above all sectional and factious prejudices . . ." and was something of an idol for the youth of the country. The daguerreotype by Mathew Brady, bottom, captures the strain and frustration of Calhoun's last years. John Randolph remarked, when Martin Van Buren won the struggle for Jacksonian favor, that "Calhoun . . . must be in Hell. . . . He is self mutilated like the Fanatic that emasculated himself." In his cold, intellectual aloofness and his absolute devotion to the cause of Southern states' rights, Calhoun, who died early in 1850, was, to Harriet Martineau, "the cast iron man who looks as if he had never been born, and never could be extinguished."

TRAIL OF TEARS

Although the Indian Removal Act of 1830 simply authorized the President to negotiate for land, Andrew Jackson's "requests" were in fact orders. Resigned to their fate, the Choctaw and Chickasaw began the long journey from the Southeast to Arkansas and Oklahoma. But the Creek, who had disastrously encountered Jackson in 1813 and 1817, knew better than to believe his promise of guaranteed territory west of the Mississippi. Standing their ground in 1832, they extracted a treaty that said "they shall be free to go or stay, as they please." Four years later, their chiefs in chains and guns at their backs, the

As the Sauk, trying to return to their home east of the Mississippi, started to cross the river at Bad Axe,

Creek joined the exodus. In 1832, the Sauk were driven from their Illinois villages and across the Mississippi, leaving possessions and food stores behind. When Chief Black Hawk sent his braves to negotiate with the military, their white flags were ignored. After several skirmishes, the desperate leader tried to lead his starving people back home, but they were stopped at the river.

That pathetic series of events, known as the Black Hawk War, cost hundreds of Indian lives. In Georgia, the peaceful Cherokee sought and won from the Supreme Court a favorable decision, to which neither the state officials nor President Jackson paid any attention. Like the other Indian tribes, the Cherokee embarked on a long journey to the West, along a "trail of tears."

the Warrior *arrived, ignored Chief Black Hawk's white flags, and opened fire, killing hundreds of Indians.*

Thomas W. Benton.

"OLD BULLION"

When Andrew Jackson remarked in 1832 that he would start hanging South Carolina nullifiers at the first sign of trouble, Senator Thomas Hart Benton added, "When Jackson begins to talk about hanging, they can begin to look for the ropes." Benton knew his man. A daily visitor to the White House, the senator from Missouri was Jackson's confidant and leader of the administration forces in the Upper House. And he knew from personal experience the intensity of Jackson's wrath: in 1813 in Nashville, after Benton had made some critical remarks about Jackson, the latter attacked him with a horsewhip and started a celebrated donnybrook during which Jackson was shot in the arm. Ten years later, Benton found himself seated beside a new Senate colleague from Tennessee—Andrew Jackson. Benton, a man of imposing physique and every bit as stubborn and egotistical as Jackson, was not cowed; neither man acknowledged the other for days. Finally Jackson, chairman of a committee of which Benton was a member, turned and said, "We are on the same committee; I will give you notice when it is necessary to attend." Benton replied guardedly, "General, make the time to suit yourself." Shortly thereafter the two shook hands, beginning a firm friendship.

An early supporter of Henry Clay, Benton backed Jackson for the Presidency in 1824, and worked for the General's election four years later. Like Jackson, Benton was a hard-money man; he led the struggle against the National Bank. "Gold and silver is the best currency for a republic," boomed Benton. A "workingman's party" and a "hard-money party" were synonymous to him. In 1831 he introduced a resolution to allow the Bank charter to expire; and it was Benton who drew up the Specie Circular of 1836. "Old Bullion," as Benton was called, fought to expunge from the Senate record a resolution censuring Jackson's conduct in the removal of deposits from Mr. Biddle's Bank. He succeeded in 1837 and gave Jackson the pen that struck the resolution from the ledger. It was Benton's bill that raised the gold-to-silver ratio to 16 to 1, generating a healthy increase in gold coinage. Ever the Democrat—or, as he himself put it with magnificent vanity, "Benton and the people, Benton and Democracy are one and the same, sir . . . ."—Benton strove to reduce Western land prices to facilitate settlement. In the latter days of his thirty-year Senate tenure he opposed the annexation of Texas on constitutional grounds and favored compromise over war in the determination of the Oregon boundary. Benton's Unionist opposition to the admission of California as anything but a free state prompted Mississippi's Senator Henry Foote to brandish a pistol at him on the Senate floor.

Benton served briefly in the House of Representatives and was a gubernatorial candidate in Missouri in 1856. He died of a wrackingly painful intestinal cancer in 1858, after completing his *Thirty Years View*, a masterful personal account of his political era. In that book's description of Van Buren's inauguration, Benton paid his final tribute to Andrew Jackson: "For once the rising was eclipsed by the setting sun."

"THE GOLDEN CALF"

I do not dislike your Bank," said Andrew Jackson in 1829 to Nicholas Biddle, president of the Bank of the United States, "any more than all banks." It had taken Jackson some time to arrive at this position: early in the 1820's, in apparent support of Biddle's institution, he had warned against the inflationary practices of the West's "printing-press banks." But now he viewed the National Bank as a monopoly, a "hydra of corruption, dangerous to our liberties," benefiting a wealthy coterie at the expense of the common man. Whatever *rapprochement* Nicholas Biddle and Jackson might have reached was precluded by presidential aspirant Henry Clay, who persuaded Biddle to lobby for an early rechartering of the Bank as campaign ammunition against Jackson in 1832. Jackson picked up the gauntlet by vetoing the recharter, and ran successfully for re-election on an anti-Bank platform. "We shall crush the Kitchen Cabinet," seethed Biddle when Jackson began to withdraw federal deposits from the doomed Bank. Biddle tightened credit and financed a congressional and editorial campaign to censure Jackson's policies. But the President stood firm: "Is Andrew Jackson to bow the knee to the golden calf?" he thundered when businessmen complained of hardship resulting from Biddle's maneuvers. "If you want relief, go to Nicholas Biddle!" Biddle eventually capitulated, and the House in 1834 passed four definitive anti-Bank resolutions. "The fate of the Bank," said Jackson, was "sealed forever."

The Greek temple, above, on Chestnut Street in Philadelphia was the seat of the Bank of the United States. From his office Nicholas Biddle controlled twenty-seven branches—and the commercial activities of the nation.

The graphic cartoon above shows pro-Bank men Henry Clay, Daniel Webster, and John Calhoun consulting on the grave illness that is causing Mother Bank to cough up her deposits. Jackson, left, looks on with pleasure.

Jackson attacks the Bank with his veto stick in the cartoon above. Van Buren, standing at center, helps kill the monster, whose many heads represent Biddle (in top hat) and directors of the state branches.

FRIENDS AND ENEMIES

NEW YORK CITY HALL ART COMMISSION

EDWARD LIVINGSTON

The friendship between Edward Livingston and Andrew Jackson began in Congress in the 1790's; from that time on, Livingston was at Jackson's side at every critical phase of the latter's career. Livingston was forced to abandon his ascent in New York City politics in 1803: deeply in debt because of dishonest subordinates, he left to practice law in New Orleans. He organized support for Jackson before the Battle of New Orleans, and became the General's aide-de-camp, confidant, and secretary. (He wrote most of the formal war dispatches.) In 1825, back in the House, Livingston completed a universally admired criminal code commissioned by the state of Louisiana. In 1828, he campaigned for Jackson, to whom he had suggested the Presidency as early as 1815; Livingston himself was elected to the Senate. His loyalty was rewarded with the post of Secretary of State in 1831. While Livingston was a moderate on the Bank issue, he agreed fully with Jackson's opposition to nullification: he wrote the Proclamation of 1832 from presidential notes. Minister to France in 1833, Livingston initiated attempts to make France pay American claims dating from the Napoleonic Wars. Britain finally mediated the controversy, but not before Jackson's saber rattling had brought the two nations to the edge of war. Livingston died in 1836.

CULVER PICTURES

AMOS KENDALL

"Amos Kendall . . . is supposed to be the moving spring of the Administration," wrote the English economist and writer Harriet Martineau in 1838, "the thinker, the planner, the doer. . . ." Kendall was indeed one of the most influential men in the Jackson fold. Jackson always rewarded friendship and service, and Kendall, editor of a powerful Kentucky newspaper, had campaigned hard for the General in 1828. When he was appointed fourth auditor of the Treasury, he approached the job "in the spirit of reform" and did in fact substantially reduce corruption in his department. But more importantly, Kendall was a member of the "Kitchen Cabinet" of confidants to whom Jackson continually turned for advice. Kendall was responsible for much of the President's paperwork and many of his speeches (annual messages, administration correspondence, the 1832 Bank veto message to Congress) and helped to found the *Globe*, the administration's official newspaper in Washington. Appointed Postmaster General in 1835, Kendall again brought about reforms but winked at Southern postmasters' suppression of antislavery mail. After some financial duress in the early 1840's, he associated himself with Samuel F. B. Morse and made enough money to spend his last decade as a political writer and philanthropist.

NICHOLAS BIDDLE

Andrew Jackson's opponent in the "Bank War" was as antithetical to him personally as he was philosophically. Nicholas Biddle, born to an old Pennsylvania family, had long displayed a precocious diversity of talent in the classics, language, literature, and diplomacy; he was a sophisticated, polished gentleman. He had been secretary of the American legation at the Court of St. James's; later, President Monroe prevailed upon him to become a director of the Bank. Only thirty-seven when he became president of the institution in 1823, Biddle believed that a strong National Bank was the foundation of a strong economy. He used the Bank's broad charter to curtail extravagant lending by state banks. Many saw him as "Czar Nicholas," while only a handful believed that his conservative policies were the best means to stabilize the nation's currency. The conflict revealed the worst in Biddle: he was arrogant ("I have been for years in the daily exercize of more personal authority than any President") and misguided, allying himself with a loser, Henry Clay. Nevertheless, Biddle's policies would have averted the depression that followed the Bank's demise in 1836. Rechartered as a state bank, the institution failed in 1841; Biddle's creditors charged fraud, but they were paid and Biddle was ultimately exonerated. He died in 1844.

JOSEPH STORY

A distinguished member of the Supreme Court since 1811, Joseph Story was the logical successor to Chief Justice John Marshall in 1835. But Story, a former member of the Massachusetts and federal legislatures, was a nationalist and a supporter of John Quincy Adams, and he was not surprised when Jackson bypassed him in favor of Roger B. Taney. Nevertheless, Story remains a dominant figure in the Court's early history. His opinions in admiralty cases during the War of 1812 became models of international law, and in 1818 he established the Court's right to judicial review of state court decisions. Upholding the broad view of the Constitution, he argued in 1837 that Congress had exclusive right to regulate state and foreign commerce. His antipathy to slavery was reflected in the *Amistad* case of 1841, in which he freed a cargo of mutinous slaves, who were then returned to Africa. Story's writings were notable for their sagacity and range of subject matter. In 1832 he began his *Commentaries on the Constitution of the United States*, which appeared in three volumes. He accepted a chair at Harvard Law School in 1829, and in his teaching, as in his writings, he played a major role in the establishment of American equity jurisprudence. Story died in Cambridge, Massachusetts, in 1845, at the age of sixty-six.

A PRESIDENT'S POSSESSIONS

Stickpin and watch

A footscraper from The Hermitage

A silver wine caddy

The President's barber chair

Jackson's banjo

A brass spittoon

DEATH OF A HERO

Hard of hearing, nearly blind in one eye, and suffering from the agonizing after-effects of a tubercular hemorrhage, Andrew Jackson lived by his own words: "I have long found that complaining never eased pain." An active interest in politics was the old Chieftain's best tonic. Jackson advised Van Buren on fiscal policies; when the latter was defeated for re-election, Jackson was roused to write, "*Beaten but I trust not conquered. . . .*" Stung by Van Buren's apostasy on Texas—whose annexation he considered vital to national security—Jackson found "Joyfull news" in "Young Hickory" Polk's nomination in 1844. A year later, Jackson's letters persuaded Sam Houston to reconsider withholding Texas from the United States. Houston arrived at The Hermitage on June 8, 1845, the day his old military colleague died. In tears, Houston led his small son to the room in which General Jackson's wasted body lay. "My son," he said, "try to remember that you have looked on the face of Andrew Jackson."

The daguerreotype at left was made shortly before Jackson died. His face and body swelling with painful dropsy, he had to spend his last days in a cushioned chair, his nights sitting up in bed. But his spirit and spark remained; his mind to the end was occupied with national affairs— Texas, Oregon, President Polk's appointments. Before he died, he said to his family and servants: "Oh, do not cry. Be good children, and we shall all meet in Heaven."

The Hermitage, near Nashville, was inspired by Mount Vernon, as the lithograph of 1848, below, indicates. Rachel selected the site of the mansion, which was completed in 1819, and tended its extensive gardens. The house, rebuilt after a fire in 1834, is now a national shrine.

FACTS IN SUMMARY: ANDREW JACKSON

CHRONOLOGY

UNITED STATES		JACKSON
Townshend Acts	1767	*Born March 15*
Declaration of Independence	1776	
Yorktown	1781	*Captured by the British*
	1784	*Begins law study*
Constitution ratified	1788	*Establishes law practice in Nashville*
Washington elected President	1789	
	1790	*Appointed attorney general of Western District of N.C.*
	1791	*Marries Rachel Robards*
		Appointed judge advocate of Davidson County militia
Washington's Farewell Address	1796	*Elected to House of Representatives*
John Adams inaugurated	1797	*Elected to U.S. Senate*
Alien and Sedition Acts	1798	*Elected judge of Tennessee superior court*
Jefferson inaugurated	1801	
	1802	*Elected major general of Tennessee militia*
Jefferson re-elected	1804	*Retires to private life*
War with Great Britain	1812	*Commands volunteer army in Creek War*
Washington burned	1814	*Defeats Creek forces at Horseshoe Bend*
		Commissioned major general of U.S. Army

	1815	*Wins Battle of New Orleans*
Rush-Bagot agreement	1817	*Commands forces in First Seminole War*
	1818	*Captures St. Marks and Pensacola in Spanish East Florida*
	1821	*Appointed governor of Florida Territory*
Monroe Doctrine	1823	*Elected to U.S. Senate*
	1824	*Fails to win majority in presidential election*
John Quincy Adams elected President by Congress	1825	
Tariff of Abominations	1828	*Elected President*
Webster-Hayne debates	1830	*Makes pro-Union toast at Jefferson Day dinner*
		Vetoes Maysville Road bill
Eaton affair	1831	*Breaks with Calhoun*
		Reorganizes Cabinet
Black Hawk War	1832	*Vetoes bill for U.S. Bank recharter*
South Carolina declares Tariff Act null and void		*Issues Proclamation to the People of South Carolina*
Calhoun resigns as Vice President		
		Re-elected President
Compromise tariff passed	1833	*Approves force bill*
		Removes deposits from the Bank of the U.S.
Second Seminole War	1835	*Narrowly escapes assassination*

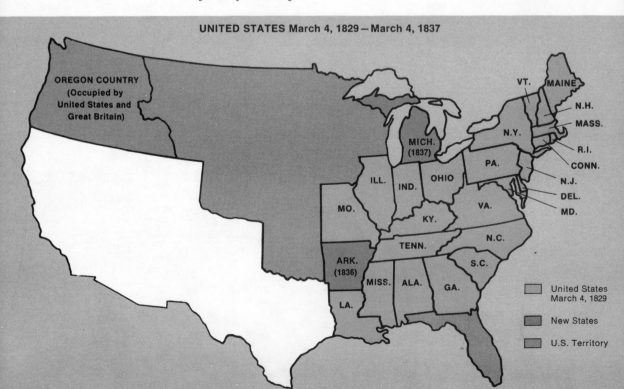

UNITED STATES March 4, 1829 — March 4, 1837

OREGON COUNTRY
(Occupied by
United States and
Great Britain)

VT. MAINE
N.H.
MASS.
N.Y.
R.I.
MICH. (1837)
CONN.
PA.
N.J.
ILL.
IND. OHIO
DEL.
MO.
VA. MD.
KY.
TENN.
N.C.
ARK. (1836)
S.C.
MISS. ALA. GA.
LA.

United States March 4, 1829

New States

U.S. Territory

Texas declares independence	1836	*Issues Specie Circular*
Siege of the Alamo		*Supports Van Buren as presidential candidate*
Van Buren elected President		
Bank panic and depression	1837	*Publishes Farewell Address*
Polk elected President	1844	*Supports Polk for Presidency*
Texas annexed	1845	*Dies June 8*

BIOGRAPHICAL FACTS

BIRTH: The Waxhaws, S.C., March 15, 1767

ANCESTRY: Scotch-Irish

FATHER: Andrew Jackson; b. Ireland; d. 1767

FATHER'S OCCUPATIONS: Linen weaver; farmer

MOTHER: Elizabeth Hutchinson Jackson; b. Ireland; d. Charleston, S.C., 1781

BROTHERS: Hugh (1762–1780); Robert (1765–1780)

WIFE: Rachel Donelson Robards; b. Halifax County, Va., June 15, 1767; d. Nashville, Tenn., Dec. 22, 1828

MARRIAGE: Natchez, Miss., August 1, 1791; second ceremony: Nashville, Tenn., Jan. 17, 1794

CHILD: Andrew Jackson, Jr. (adopted) (1810–?)

HOME: The Hermitage, Nashville, Tenn.

EDUCATION: Attended public schools; studied law in Salisbury, S.C.

RELIGIOUS AFFILIATION: Presbyterian

OCCUPATIONS BEFORE PRESIDENCY: Lawyer; soldier; politician

MILITARY SERVICE: Judge advocate of Davidson County militia (c. 1791); major general of Tennessee militia (1802–1812); major general of U.S. Army (1814–1821)

PRE-PRESIDENTIAL OFFICES: Attorney General of Western District of N.C.; Delegate to Tennessee State Constitutional Convention; Member of U.S. House of Representatives; Member of U.S. Senate; Tennessee Supreme Court Judge; Governor of Florida Territory

AGE AT INAUGURATION: 61

DEATH: Nashville, Tenn., June 8, 1845

PLACE OF BURIAL: The Hermitage, Nashville, Tenn.

ELECTION OF 1828

CANDIDATES	ELECTORAL VOTE	POPULAR VOTE
Andrew Jackson Democratic	178	647,286
John Quincy Adams National Republican	83	508,064

FIRST ADMINISTRATION

INAUGURATION: March 4, 1829; the Capitol, Washington, D.C.

VICE PRESIDENT: John Calhoun (resigned Dec., 1832)

SECRETARY OF STATE: Martin Van Buren; Edward Livingston (from May 24, 1831)

SECRETARY OF THE TREASURY: Samuel D. Ingham; Louis McLane (from Aug. 8, 1831)

SECRETARY OF WAR: John H. Eaton; Lewis Cass (from Aug. 8, 1831)

ATTORNEY GENERAL: John M. Berrien; Roger B. Taney (from July 20, 1831)

POSTMASTER GENERAL: John McLean; William T. Barry (from April 6, 1829)

SECRETARY OF THE NAVY: John Branch; Levi Woodbury (from May 23, 1831)

SUPREME COURT APPOINTMENTS: John McLean (1829); Henry Baldwin (1830)

21st CONGRESS (March 4, 1829–March 4, 1831):
Senate: 26 Democrats; 22 National Republicans
House: 139 Democrats; 74 National Republicans

22nd CONGRESS (March 4, 1831–March 4, 1833):
Senate: 25 Democrats; 21 National Republicans; 2 Others
House: 141 Democrats; 58 National Republicans; 14 Others

ELECTION OF 1832

CANDIDATES	ELECTORAL VOTE	POPULAR VOTE
Andrew Jackson Democratic	219	687,502
Henry Clay National Republican	49	530,189
John Floyd Nullifier	11	
William Wirt Antimasonic	7	

SECOND ADMINISTRATION

INAUGURATION: March 4, 1833; House of Representatives, Washington, D.C.

VICE PRESIDENT: Martin Van Buren

SECRETARY OF STATE: Edward Livingston; Louis McLane (from May 29, 1833); John Forsyth (from July 1, 1834)

SECRETARY OF THE TREASURY: Louis McLane; William J. Duane (from June 1, 1833); Roger B. Taney (from Sept. 23, 1833); Levi Woodbury (from July 1, 1834)

SECRETARY OF WAR: Lewis Cass

ATTORNEY GENERAL: Roger B. Taney; Benjamin F. Butler (from Nov. 18, 1833)

POSTMASTER GENERAL: William T. Barry; Amos Kendall (from May 1, 1835)

SECRETARY OF THE NAVY: Levi Woodbury; Mahlon Dickerson (from June 30, 1834)

SUPREME COURT APPOINTMENTS: James M. Wayne (1835); Roger B. Taney, Chief Justice (1836); Philip P. Barbour (1836)

23rd CONGRESS (March 4, 1833–March 4, 1835):
Senate: 20 Democrats; 20 National Republicans; 8 Others
House: 147 Democrats; 53 Antimasons; 60 Others

24th CONGRESS (March 4, 1835–March 4, 1837):
Senate: 27 Democrats; 25 Whigs
House: 145 Democrats; 98 Whigs

STATES ADMITTED: Arkansas (1836); Michigan (1837)

MARTIN VAN BUREN

In succeeding Andrew Jackson as President, Martin Van Buren—in a commanding sense—succeeded himself in the White House. Van Buren was, after all, the prime architect of the Democratic party structure that helped to elect Jackson. He managed Old Hickory's campaign and delivered the support of New York's powerful machine. After the election, he served Jackson as Secretary of State, Vice President, phrasemaker, and confidant. Their relationship was so close that a tired Jackson once considered resigning from the Presidency during his second term, permitting Van Buren to replace him. In short, there would have been no President Jackson, as we know him, without Martin Van Buren.

As Arthur M. Schlesinger, Jr., has written, "Van Buren's understanding of the new functions of public opinion, as well as of Congress, furnished the practical mechanisms which transformed Jackson's extraordinary popularity into the instruments of power. . . . Without them, the gains of Jacksonian democracy would have been impossible." Van Buren lacked Washington's grandeur, Jackson's dash, and Jefferson's patrician intellect. But for all his rough edges and weaknesses, he grasped intuitively three central political facts of the time: that Congress had declined in power and influence; that a stronger judiciary had emerged; and, pre-eminently, that executive power was to be gained by popular persuasion rather than by presidential pleading with Congress. The common man controlled the nation now, and the masses needed to be told the whys and hows of political processes. It was to the development of this presidential method, especially in Jackson's two terms, that Martin Van Buren applied his great political talent. He became in the process the United States' first systematic national politician.

Born on December 5, 1782, in the village of Kinderhook in New York's Co-

G. P. A. Healy's portrait of Van Buren hangs in the White House.

lumbia County, he was the son of Abraham and Maria (Hoes) Van Buren, both Dutch. Although a more sophisticated Van Buren would suggest in post-presidential retirement that his ancestors might have been nobles, his father was, in fact, a truck farmer and tavern keeper who fought in the Revolution, served as Kinderhook town clerk, raised his son in the Dutch Reformed Church, and owned slaves.

Traditionally, American Presidents lisp republican principles from their trundle beds and seem destined at twelve to command ships of state. Not so Van Buren. His education was limited to a few years at a provincial academy, and he openly confessed to a secondary intellect. He preferred light reading to heavy, and action to abstraction. At some point, however, he acquired a penchant for law and polemics, and at fourteen entered the law firm of Francis Silvester, a Federalist. He swept floors, served as scrivener, studied law, and, as a burgeoning Republican, talked himself out of a job. Van Buren then moved to New York City, where he campaigned for Jefferson in 1800—his political baptism—and pursued his law career under attorney William P. Van Ness, a disciple of Aaron Burr.

Little Van, so named because he was only five feet six inches tall, returned to Kinderhook, was admitted to the bar in 1803, and began a systematic ascent to the summits of local, state, and national power. He kept a strict and circumspect counsel, avoiding controversial commitments and uniting antagonistic factions whenever possible. He married a distant kinswoman, Hannah Hoes, on February 21, 1807 (she died twelve years later), and fathered four sons, one of whom, John, would share some of his father's distinction and promise as a leader in the Free-Soil movement. Another son, Abraham, was to serve during his father's Presidency as a White House secretary.

By 1808, the truck farmer's son was surrogate of Columbia County. In 1812, he was elected—on an anti-U.S. Bank platform—to the state senate. There he supported the War of 1812, the construction of the lucra-

tive Erie Canal, and the revision of New York State's constitution. Van Buren also sponsored a bill to abolish imprisonment for debt—one of the first legislators to do so in the United States.

During his second term as state senator, Van Buren was appointed New York State attorney general, and successfully prosecuted General William Hull for cowardice and neglect of duty in surrendering Detroit to the British in the War of 1812; Hull's sentence, however, was remanded by President Madison.

Van Buren slowly assumed command of New York's Republican "Bucktail" wing, which was formally committed to a strict adherence to Jeffersonian principles and opposed to DeWitt Clinton's tolerance for Federalists. In securing control of the Bucktails, Van Buren learned a lesson that would serve him well in the White House: the great advantage of a friendly press. His organ in Albany was the *Argus*, edited by hand-picked Van Buren disciples. Without a paper managed by "a sound, practicable, and above all discreet republican," he stated with candor, "we may hang our harps on the willows." In Washington, Francis Blair's friendly *Globe* would serve Van Buren's purposes with comparable efficiency.

Van Buren was elected to the United States Senate in 1821. Before leaving for Washington, however, he made certain that the New York sheep would not play while the "Red Fox of Kinderhook" (another of his many nicknames) was away: he sealed an already tightly capped party machine—since known as the Albany Regency. Its structural informality notwithstanding, the Regency governed political patronage, defined party policy, ran campaigns, and—after freewheeling, secret party caucuses—assured its members' public loyalty with the threat of prompt removal from office for any departure from the party line. Working in tandem with Tammany Hall in New York City, the Regency assured Martin Van Buren's hegemony in the state, which from 1830 to 1860 contained one-seventh of the population of the United States.

250

In 1824 Van Buren led William H. Crawford's unsuccessful presidential campaign against John Quincy Adams, Henry Clay, and—of all people—Andrew Jackson. But Van Buren swiftly learned the lessons of Adams' victory and carefully moved to unify the supporters of Jackson, Calhoun, and Crawford into a viable political force. The objective for 1828: an appealing synthesis of Jackson's popularity and Jefferson's principles, packaged and sold by a new Democratic party. To sew up New York's pivotal vote for the General, Van Buren himself gave up his Senate seat to run for governor of New York, thus adding his own popular name to the ticket.

Van Buren's tactical coalition won. It was a mean campaign, and his lieutenants sank low to win. It was a contest, they said, between "John Quincy Adams, who can write" and "Andrew Jackson, who can fight." This unfair campaign technique would one day help to unseat Van Buren himself as President. But it worked for Old Hickory, even though the Adams forces lowered their campaign to the same level. The General was in the White House.

Van Buren was back in Albany—but only for a short time. In two and a half months, he resigned as governor and was promptly named Jackson's Secretary of State. He was easily the most powerful man in either the official or "Kitchen Cabinet." As Secretary of State, Van Buren's achievements were impressive. The world's chancelleries had been initially appalled by the mercurial and crotchety frontier President, and Van Buren —cordial, discreet, and immaculate—buffered the fray. A French minister would praise Van Buren's "certain ease, which makes him superior, as a man of the world, to those of his compatriots I have seen until now." When Washington Irving was in the diplomatic corps, he noted that Van Buren was "one of the gentlest and most amiable men I have ever met with." Highly respected in London, Van Buren reached a settlement with the Crown on West Indian trade; he also negotiated American access to the Black Sea with Turkey and persuaded

RICHARD M. JOHNSON

After receiving only a plurality in the election of 1836, Richard Mentor Johnson became the sole Vice President ever elected by the Senate. Like Van Buren, he had been Jackson's personal choice, but in contrast to the suave Van Buren, Johnson was a frontiersman, born in Kentucky in 1780. He was a brilliant soldier and an eccentric and careless dresser. Thus he brought to the ticket an appeal to the backwoods vote that the fastidious Van Buren did not have. Although Johnson had been prominent in both the Kentucky and national legislatures, urging government-sponsored education, he was an inconspicuous Vice President. But he became a problem for his party in 1840. When the Democrats nominated the unmarried congressman in 1836, they knew that he was the father of two daughters by a mulatto girl. Not until 1840 did Southern opposition to him solidify, and then even Jackson thought Johnson would be "dead wait [sic]" on the ticket. Johnson was not renominated, but he ran anyway. The Whig campaign of 1840 centered on Harrison's victories over the Indians, and inadvertently reminded the voters that Johnson had allegedly killed Tecumseh during the Battle of the Thames. Barnstorming throughout the nation to the chant, "Rumpsey dumpsey, Colonel Johnson shot Tecumseh," he displayed his battle scars wherever he went. But the Democratic ticket was defeated and Johnson retired.

the French to pay American damage claims from the Napoleonic Wars.

But Van Buren's importance to Jackson, even as Secretary of State, remained primarily political. He and Jackson agreed that only with the support of a strong political party could the President exercise effective leadership. To build this base of power, the lessons learned in Albany were systematically applied. There was no such thing as nonpartisanship: to the faithful belonged the jobs, and the key was patronage. Largely administered by Van Buren, the spoils system was dangled over the heads of the politically uncertain. "We give no reasons for our removals," said Van Buren, and the opposition seized on the patronage concept to paint a corrupt portrait of the administration. Actually, the number of dismissals of government employees was relatively modest—estimates range from one-eleventh to one-eighth, about the same proportion that Jefferson had removed.

With equal intensity, Van Buren pressed hard for Jackson's legislation in Congress. He drafted the General's veto of Congress' bill authorizing federal investment in the sixty-mile Maysville Road in Kentucky. Such support, Van Buren argued, was an unconstitutional federal intrusion in state affairs—even if the state wanted the intrusion. Most of the time, however, Martin Van Buren preferred to operate outside of congressional chambers. In the corridors, in drawing rooms, in his offices, he wheeled and dealt, playing faction against faction, molding consensus toward his own ends, earning his titles "Red Fox" and "Little Magician."

Among his impressive political tricks was his disposal of Vice President Calhoun as a rival for succession to the Presidency. Like all good tricks, it was simply executed. In 1830 Jackson and Calhoun had clashed over the principle of nullification, which the Vice President had espoused. Van Buren dutifully reminded Old Hickory that Calhoun had also opposed Jackson's military intervention in Florida in 1818—and not without point, for Calhoun had assured General Jackson that he had supported the action.

In the famed Eaton affair, the political war escalated. Calhoun's wife and those of most Cabinet members had ostracized Secretary of War and Mrs. Eaton, persuaded that the couple had been living together long before the death of Mrs. Eaton's first husband. No doubt because his own wife, Rachel, had suffered gravely at the hands of rumormongers, Jackson decreed Peggy Eaton's virtue and championed her cause. But Cabinet husbands and wives remained undissuaded despite the suspension of Cabinet meetings by Jackson, who demanded that Peggy be invited to the social events of the Capital. In the ensuing stalemate the President found himself hog-tied. He could not provide the Whigs with a critical issue by firing all Calhoun men in his Cabinet, but neither could he capitulate and accept Eaton's resignation. Van Buren, who had valued the Eatons' friendship, reached into his magic hat and pulled out his own resignation! Jackson was nonplused until Old Kinderhook explained that his resignation as an apparent neutral in the imbroglio would make it possible for the entire Cabinet to resign. Van Buren's strategy worked; Eaton withdrew and Jackson ordered the rest of the Cabinet to follow suit. The Eaton embarrassment was thus cleverly resolved, and in the process Martin Van Buren earned himself the Vice Presidency in 1832.

In the interim Little Van served as minister to Great Britain while Congress was in recess. But when the reconvened Senate was asked to confirm his appointment, Calhoun openly opposed it. The Senate's tie vote gave him his opportunity for revenge: as Vice President he had the power to break the tie, and he gleefully voted Nay. Triumphant, he sneered: "It will kill him dead, sir, kill him dead. He will never kick, sir, never kick." But Senator Thomas Hart Benton could not agree. To a Calhoun lieutenant sitting beside him Benton observed: "You have broken a minister, and elected a Vice President." Benton was right. An angry Jackson chose Van Buren as his running mate in 1832, and in 1835 named him his successor in the White House.

In November, 1836, "Old Kinderhook" (Van Buren's campaign initials gave birth to the expression "O.K."), running on a Jacksonian platform of democracy versus aristocracy, was elected the eighth President of the United States. His chief rival was a general named William Henry Harrison.

It was a wild—and cruel—political era. As Vice President, Van Buren had felt the need to hide two pistols beneath his jacket. In the campaign of 1836, the redoubtable William Seward called Van Buren "a crawling reptile, whose only claim was that he had inveigled the confidence of a credulous, blind, dotard, old man." Even the staid John Quincy Adams recorded in his diary as perhaps credible a rumor that Van Buren was the illegitimate son of Aaron Burr. To his detractors, Van Buren was the American Talleyrand, devious, hypocritical, professionally noncommittal. "The searching look of his keen eyes," observed one hostile contemporary, "showed that he believed, with Talleyrand, that language was given to conceal thought." John Randolph said of Van Buren: "He rowed to his object with muffled oars." The mud was not restricted to one camp, however. Van Buren's own party organ, the *Globe*, had itself pilloried General Harrison as a "superannuated old woman . . . a red petticoat general" and referred to him as "the hero of forty defeats."

Seminole Indians attack a federal fort in Florida in the 1837 lithograph above. They refused to be moved west and fought fiercely for seven years.

Yet despite all the invective, Martin Van Buren entered the White House with roseate good cheer. In his Inaugural Address in March, 1837, he recalled that he was the first President born after the Revolution began; "whilst I contemplate with grateful reverence that memorable event," he said, "I feel that I belong to a later age. . . ." Then, he addressed himself to the issues of the time, revealing that the inclinations of the New York politician would not be discarded by the new Chief Executive. To help unify the Democratic party, he dismissed Southern nullification of federal law as an embarrassment," a "partial and temporary evil," and blandly appealed for the old caucus consensus, for "free and fearless discussion, blended with unimpaired fraternal feeling." On the eve of one of America's worst depressions, he assured the nation that prosperity was now "perfectly secured." Faced already with angry rumblings of secession, he hailed the Founding Fathers' respect for "distinct sovereignties" within the nation and for "institutions peculiar to the various portions" of the country. But he urged that the unrest of Southerners not be "exaggerated through sinister designs. . . ."

"I must go into the Presidential chair," Jackson's heir proclaimed, "the inflexible and uncompromising opponent of every attempt on the part of Congress to abolish slavery in the District of Columbia against the wishes of the slaveholding States, and also with a determination equally decided to resist the slightest interference with it in the States where it exists." Promising to veto any bill "conflicting with these views," Van Buren urged "forbearance" with "the delicacy of this subject [slavery]." He assured the nation that his beliefs were "in accordance with the spirit that actuated the venerated fathers of the Republic. . . ." "I throw myself without fear on [the country's] justice and its kindness," he said. "May her ways be ways of pleasantness and all her paths be peace."

But the nation's ways were not pleasant, nor was America kind—or particularly just —to the chief Albany regent. Within days of his accession, Van Buren faced a major na-

tional depression—the Panic of 1837—which was to plague his administration for the length of its days. Ironically, the Panic was largely due to the execution of and opposition to Jackson's Specie Circular. "In destroying the bank," Schlesinger writes, "Jackson had removed a valuable brake on credit expansion; and in sponsoring the system of [federal] deposit in state banks, he had accelerated the tendencies toward inflation."

The basic cause of the crash was business' defiance of Jackson's hard-money policy in overextending paper credit to finance the boom in land speculation, manufacturing, transportation, and banking that had begun under Adams. Hard money was withdrawn en masse from the banks to pay for Western lands. The wheat crop of 1836 failed badly. The price of cotton fell by almost one-half. Food and fuel prices and rents soared, sometimes doubled. New Yorkers rioted over the cost of flour. Banks and businesses collapsed

Also struck by a depression, England and France asked Van Buren for payment of debts in hard money (above). But their reduction of American imports and tightened credit had already worsened the specie shortage here.

under pressure from England and Europe for repayment of short-term loans precisely when hard-money deposits were being depleted. Suffering was rife, poorhouses were crowded. The government alone lost nine million dollars in the failure of state banks. Nearly every bank in the country suspended specie payments.

By May, 1837, President Van Buren could temporize no longer. He summoned Congress into special session to deal with the Panic. His own solutions: stand fast for hard money; remove the federal deposits from all banks, state and national; establish an independent treasury that would wrest control of the government from the moneyed class. But a predictable coalition of state banking interests, Whigs, and conservative Democrats prevented passage of his Independent Treasury bill. Not until 1840, the last year of his administration, did the bill pass. Van Buren would hail its passage as a "Second Declaration of Independence," and would delight in having won Jackson's battle with Nicholas Biddle, but the Independent Treasury, in fact, would not be established on a permanent basis until 1846.

Van Buren's struggle for an Independent Treasury was by no means his only achievement as President. Despite his repeated belief that the federal government had no constitutional right to intervene in the economy, he issued in March, 1840, an Executive Order limiting to a ten-hour day the work of all laborers on federal projects. In 1837, Canada seized in American waters the U.S. steamer *Caroline*, which was illegally carrying supplies to the insurgents in a Canadian uprising. Van Buren defied both British bluster and American jingoist cries for vengeance by disarming intervening American zealots and smoothing the Crown's ruffled feathers. Similarly, in 1840, when Maine citizens clashed with Canadians over the boundary of the Northeast United States, Van Buren quietly ended the conflict and initiated a diplomatic dialogue concluded in the Webster-Ashburton Treaty of 1842.

Despite these displays of executive authority, the image of Van Buren as an eva-sive manipulator, unwilling to take an unpopular stand, remained. Even Jackson lost patience with his old alter ego when Van Buren, fearing war with Mexico, opposed both Jackson and Sam Houston on the annexation of Texas. Old Hickory looked increasingly to James K. Polk as a more tractable heir to his tradition.

Van Buren's ambivalence was due not only to political machination but equally to a highly limited view of the presidential and federal roles in the life of the nation and to a fundamentalist approach to the principles of Jefferson. This interpretation of Jeffersonianism was restricted to an embrace of states' rights as a screen for federal inaction and of limited government to perpetuate the status quo. Van Buren's view of the Constitution was ambiguous. On the one hand, he anointed it as "a sacred instrument," while on the other, he defied one of its fundamental principles by favoring an elective judiciary. He approved of Congress' explicit right to collect taxes, but he felt that the Constitution gave Congress no authority to spend these taxes—even after all basic expenses of government had been met —on internal improvements: public roads, schools, or canals. He also believed that the federal government had no constitutional right to correct inequities, resolve crises, or influence events. His fight for the Independent Treasury excepted, Van Buren's administration was the apotheosis of laissez-faire government. In international affairs, he declared his opposition to "all forms of . . . alliances." Precedents set in our foreign relations, he explained, left "little to [his] discretion, unless, indeed, I were willing to run counter to the lights of experience and the known opinions of my constituents." Historians also agree that his appointments, even on the highest levels, were capricious and inept. A "little magician" in securing and sustaining power for others, Van Buren himself was weak in the exercise of power.

Van Buren's perennial fence-sitting earned him enemies everywhere. He was blamed, as Hoover would be blamed, not only for the depression during his administration but for failure to combat it head on. He was regarded as proslavery in the North and antislavery in the South. And despite his victory over Biddle and the announcement of an Independent Treasury, he faced, in the campaign of 1840, a most hostile nation.

The tone of the campaign—one of the most visceral in American history—was sounded by Pennsylvania Congressman Charles Ogle in the House of Representatives on April 14, 1840. Commenting on a routine appropriation of $3,665 for White House maintenance and repairs, Ogle began an impassioned appeal for the election of William Henry Harrison, with an incredible assault on the person of the President. Van Buren, declared Ogle, wore the same perfume fancied by Queen Victoria, actually preferred Madeira to hard cider, and used "Fanny Kemble green glass finger cups." Moreover, Ogle raged on, the President had purchased—in Europe of all places—Brussels carpets, "dazzling foreign ornaments," French tabo-rets for royal audiences, and other "woman-ish" contrivances. Van Buren, he said, actually slept in a Louis XV bed and used "gold-framed mirrors 'as big as a barn door' to behold his plain Republican self."

Reigning from his "royal establishment" at the cost of the nation, Ogle said, Van Buren looked down upon the people as "suckers" and "fawning spaniels" as he luxuriated in "sloth and effeminacy." The cost of three White House curtains alone, Ogle maintained, would build at least three goodly log cabins with money to spare to "treat the folks who came to the *raisin*' with as much HARD CIDER as they can stow away under the belts of their linsey-woolsey hunting shirts."

The campaign was on. Like the Democrats in 1828, the Whigs nominated a military hero, William Henry Harrison. And also like the Democrats in 1828, the Whigs equated refinement with sexual aberration and intellect with weakness.

In contrast to Van Buren's sybaritic and royal splendor, Harrison was hailed as a frontier messiah, champion of the little people of whom God in His wisdom had

made so many. When the votes were counted, it was found that many conservative Democrats had defected to the Whigs, and Old Tippecanoe had won by a plurality of 150,-000 in a smashing electoral victory of 234 votes to 60. Van Buren even lost his own state, New York.

Of the Presidency, Van Buren said, agreeing with Jefferson, that "the two happiest days of his life were those of his entrance upon the office and of his surrender of it." He returned to Kinderhook, moving into "Lindenwald," a remodeled Italo-Gothic mansion. In 1844, after turning down President Tyler's politically motivated offer of a seat on the Supreme Court, Van Buren tried for the Democratic presidential nomination, but failed because of his continued opposition to the annexation of Texas, a slave state. In 1848, he was renominated by antislavery Democrats (the "Barnburners") in coalition with Free-Soilers and liberal Whigs. The Democrats nominated Lewis Cass; the Whigs, Zachary Taylor. With the New York Democrats thus split, Taylor carried the state and won the election. In the course of the 1848 campaign, Van Buren finally concluded that slavery and freedom could not coexist and wrote a moving appeal for free soil with his son John and future presidential candidate Samuel Tilden.

In retirement, besides playing patroon at Lindenwald, Van Buren traveled for several years in Europe. Without fear of political retribution, he was able to poke around ancestral Dutch towns and indulge himself in the purchase of the European finery he enjoyed so much. At the Villa Falangola in Sorrento, Italy, in 1854, the seventy-one-year-old former Chief Executive wrote his story for his countrymen.

Back in Kinderhook, Van Buren seethed over the policies of Presidents Pierce and Buchanan. In 1861, mourning the commencement of the Civil War, he expressed his confidence in Abraham Lincoln. Plagued by asthma for many months, Martin Van Buren died in the second year of the conflict, on July 29, 1862.

—WILSON SULLIVAN

M Van Buren

A PICTURE PORTFOLIO

*On this 1836 campaign item, candidate Martin Van Buren
is encircled in a star surrounded by a star-studded horseshoe.*

FROM THE WARDS
TO THE WHITE HOUSE

His soldierly posture and immaculate grooming made Martin Van Buren appear taller than his 5 feet 6 inches. This portrait was painted when he was governor of New York, in 1829, by Henry Inman. The building in the background is the Albany capitol.

Martin Van Buren was as shrewd, manipulating, and intensely partisan a politician as his reputation suggested. But if he was indeed the prototype of the latter-day ward heeler, he differed from the Tweeds and Pendergasts of American history because he sought and won power for himself through high elected office, not by managing the careers of others. Fighting tooth and nail in political arenas, he was, at the same time, as honest as he was intriguing, as generous in his public relations as he was wily in his politics. He could not understand why he should not be able to maintain personal friendships with political enemies; it was usually his opponents, not he, who confused the two.

As a staunch young Republican, he learned law in the office of an equally staunch Federalist. After battling his way to the leadership of New York State's Republican organization, he managed, in 1820, to have a Republican legislature elected in the same year that Federalist DeWitt Clinton was reelected governor. A year later, he went to Washington as a senator, and in 1827 he joined the political camp of General Andrew Jackson. Van Buren's own power had been solidified by the Albany *Argus*, a partisan newspaper owned in part by his brother-in-law; and the senator, who was perhaps the first American politician to understand the importance of a friendly press, began employing the *Argus* to strengthen Jackson's position in the Northeast. To help the General carry New York in the presidential election of 1828, Van Buren ran for governor. Both men won, and Van Buren, after just two and a half months in Albany, returned to Washington as Jackson's Secretary of State and, next, as his Vice President. Eight years later, Van Buren became the eighth President of the United States.

The rejected Minister,
*We never can make him President,
without first making him Vice-president.*
Vide webb.

In the struggle for power between John C. Calhoun and Martin Van Buren during Jackson's first administration, the Little Magician from New York always managed to turn the Vice President's triumphs into defeats. When Calhoun cast the deciding vote in the Senate against the appointment of Van Buren as minister to England, the Southerner thought that he had disposed of Van Buren once and for all. But as the cartoon at left indicates, the rejected minister came home to take the Vice Presidency away from Calhoun in 1832 and to become Jackson's obvious heir apparent. In 1837, after Van Buren had beaten Whig candidates William Henry Harrison, Hugh L. White, and Daniel Webster, Calhoun had to watch the scene depicted below: Van Buren's inauguration.

The snuffbox above, decorated with an idealized portrait of presidential candidate Martin Van Buren, was a souvenir of the campaign of 1836.

Nothing in the Little Magician's bag of tricks was equal to the crisis that burst in his face a few weeks after he took office. Andrew Jackson's execution of the Bank of the United States and the resulting Specie Circular of 1836—which demanded payment in hard money for all government lands—led to the Panic of 1837. The cartoon at right makes it clear that Old Hickory (Lady Macbeth) and his allies (a Southern planter who dealt in specie anyway and a city workingman who had no money and could also afford to be anti-Bank) were the real assassins of commerce, but its ghost haunts not them but Van Buren. While it may have been true that the new President was almost as frightened as he appears here, he was not helpless; and when some of his advisers suggested that he rescind the Specie Circular, Van Buren resisted the temptation. He labored, instead, to establish a permanent arrangement under which the nation's finances could be conducted: an Independent Treasury.

TROUBLED TIMES

Triggered by Jackson's victory over the National Bank, a depression engulfed the country during Van Buren's administration. "The less government interferes with private pursuits the better for the general prosperity," the President said; and instead of suggesting ways to end the depression, he turned his energies to winning passage of his Independent Treasury bill, under which all federal funds would be kept in government vaults, not in state or

private banks. The bill passed in 1840, but in the meantime even foreign affairs were affected by the financial problems. American inability to pay debts to creditors worsened Anglo-American relations, which were already tense due to the efforts of United States citizens to aid Canadian insurrectionists. In 1837, on the Niagara River, Canadian troops seized an American ship, the *Caroline*, which was bringing arms to the rebels. One American was killed, and in response to patriotic indignation, Van Buren sent troops to the border. Despite the President's pleas for neutrality in Canadian troubles, further incidents kept tensions high. Then, in 1839, Canadians began cutting timber in the Aroostook area, claimed by Maine. War seemed likely until Van Buren dispatched Winfield Scott to arrange a truce. Anglo-American differences were not settled until 1842, but by then Tyler, not Van Buren, was the occupant of the White House.

NO HOG AND HOMINY

When Martin Van Buren became President, he practiced what he had always preached: that political enemies could be personal friends. A long-time gourmet, the Chief Executive employed an English chef and, with characteristic generosity, invited Whig and Jacksonian alike

Soon after the widower-President and his four sons moved into the White House, Dolley Madison came to call. Appalled by the conspicuous absence of a woman, the former First Lady turned matchmaker and sent for her pretty young South Carolina cousin, Angelica Singleton, who was just the right age for Abraham, Van Buren's eldest son. Less than a year later, Washington had its hostess. In the portrait by Henry Inman above, Angelica stands alongside a bust of the President.

to frequent dinner parties, kept small to ensure the quality of the cuisine. Even John Calhoun and Henry Clay came often. Complimenting their host, his comradely enemies prepared to stab his political back—fair play according to Van Buren's own standards. What, his opponents asked publicly, was the meaning of all these exclusive little dinners? Was this elegant host who allegedly redecorated the Executive Mansion with European finery really a Democrat? A good American, they charged, was not even allowed in the White House if his shoes were muddy. The Whigs, said a Whig, were happy with "fried meat and gravy, or hog and hominy," and, of course, hard cider. Van Buren had no complaint: these were the tactics he had himself developed to elect Andrew Jackson to the Presidency in 1828. Turned against him in 1840, they beat him.

The romanticized etching above of Tiber Creek and the southern grounds of the White House was made in 1839 or 1840. About forty years later, the creek was filled in and was transformed into Constitution Avenue.

VOICES OF REFORM

HORACE MANN

"Be ashamed to die," said Horace Mann, "until you have won some victory for humanity." Dedicated to the cause of education, Mann was in the forefront of the humanitarian reform movement during the Van Buren years. Born in poverty in Franklin, Massachusetts, his formative years were marked by repression and frustration. The masters at his district school were often brutal and ignorant, and he was unable to attend even those sessions for more than a few weeks a year. In 1816, at twenty, he prepared himself for college in only six months with the aid of an itinerant tutor; he graduated from Brown in 1819. His reputation as a brilliant lawyer won him a seat in the state legislature in 1827; he later became president of the senate. When in 1837 he was offered the newly established post of secretary of the State Board of Education, he readily accepted. In twelve years he transformed the Massachusetts public school system. Educational appropriations and teachers' salaries were more than doubled, a six-month minimum school year was instituted, fifty new high schools were built, and the nation's first teacher training schools were organized. Until his death in 1859, Mann continued to work for education reforms while serving as congressman, professor, and the president of Antioch College.

MARY LYON

Two months before Martin Van Buren's election to the Presidency in 1836, Mary Lyon predicted: "This will be an era in female education." Born in 1797 in Massachusetts, where she attended the academies at Ashfield and Amherst, Mary Lyon was an indefatigable champion of education for women. At twenty-four, her passion for learning unsatisfied, she entered a seminary at Byfield run by the Reverend Joseph Emerson. Inspired by his dedication to female scholarship, she began her teaching career at Ashfield and later taught at a girls' school in Ipswich. During thirteen years of teaching, she formulated a plan for a women's college that would attract the rich and at the same time be "so economical that people in very moderate circumstances would be equally and as fully accommodated." In 1834 she persuaded a group of influential men to help finance such an institution, and three years later the doors were opened at Mount Holyoke Seminary—the nation's first permanent institution of higher education for women. Its founder's influence was evident in a curriculum strongly oriented to the arts and sciences. When Mary Lyon died in 1849, she left behind an established institution that reflected her theories of excellence in the physical and spiritual—as well as the intellectual—training of American women.

WILLIAM ELLERY CHANNING

"He breathed into theology a humane spirit," reads the inscription on William Ellery Channing's statue in the Public Garden of Boston. When the young pastor rebelled against the strictures of the New England Calvinism in which he was reared, it was not to found a new religious sect, but "to escape the narrow walls of a particular church. . . ." Nonetheless, when the Unitarian Church evolved around the principles of his humanitarian philosophy, Channing became its acknowledged leader and unofficial spokesman. Ordained in 1803 at the age of twenty-three, he gained a wide following as pastor of Boston's Federal Street Church, where he remained until his death in 1842. An eloquent speaker of exceptional power, he preached a liberal doctrine asserting the inherent dignity and perfectibility of mankind. In 1819, he defined and defended the position of the Unitarian movement, and the following year organized the Berry Street Conference, from which the American Unitarian Association was formed in 1825. A prolific writer and dedicated humanist, Channing exerted his influence not only on religion, but on politics, on education, and particularly on American literature. Among the many writers who acknowledged their indebtedness to Channing were Emerson, Longfellow, Bryant, Lowell, and Holmes.

WILLIAM LLOYD GARRISON

William Lloyd Garrison of Massachusetts was the most uncompromising abolitionist of his day. "I hate slavery," he said, "as I hate nothing else in this world. It is not only a crime, but the sum of all criminality." In 1831, the twenty-five-year-old editor founded his famous weekly, the *Liberator*, with the promise "*I will be heard.*" For thirty-five years—through Van Buren's administration and on to the end of the Civil War—its pages rang out in a torrent of invective against the evils of slavery and oppression. In 1833, the young reformer helped to found the American Anti-Slavery Society and soon became its president and most vociferous defender. Inspiring an antipathy as broad and active as his following, he narrowly escaped with his life when, in 1835, an angry mob seized him and dragged him through the streets with a rope around his neck. Far from seeking conciliation with his adversaries of the South, Garrison publicly advocated disunion and denounced the Compromise of 1850 as a "hollow bargain for the North." At the end of the Civil War in 1865, the aging abolitionist turned his full energies to other reforms. In the remaining fourteen years of his life, Garrison fought vigorously for woman suffrage, the prohibition of liquor, the elimination of prostitution, and belated justice for the Indians of the United States.

DISAPPOINTMENTS

In 1848, Martin Van Buren bolted the Democratic party and ran for the Presidency on the Free-Soil ticket. Eight years earlier, as Whigs throughout the nation gleefully chanted "Van is a used-up man," he had lost the office to William Henry Harrison. But he had subsequently toured the West and Southwest, demonstrating that he was not at all used up and tightening his seemingly secure grip on the 1844 nomination. At the last minute, however, his refusal to come out unequivocally for the annexation of Texas had cost him the nomination, and James Polk had won the candidacy and the Presidency. But in the next four years, the old habits of hesitation and fence-sitting were replaced by candor and forcefulness, as Van Buren clearly expressed his opinion that slavery should not be extended. When, in 1848, the Democrats nominated Lewis Cass, the old Barnburner wing of the party joined with other antislavery groups to form the Free-Soil party, and Van Buren was named to head its ticket. He won enough votes in New York to deprive Cass of victory in a close race with Zachary Taylor. In the last years of his life, Van Buren broke his own precedent of not allowing political differences to affect his personal relationships; he staunchly refused to have anything to do with President James Buchanan because of the latter's failure to avert the Civil War.

The cartoon above reminded voters in 1848 of the Free-Soil candidate's legendary political straddling—a posture that Martin Van Buren had largely abandoned. The daguerreotype opposite may have been made that year.

FACTS IN SUMMARY: MARTIN VAN BUREN

CHRONOLOGY

UNITED STATES		VAN BUREN
Peace negotiations begin in Paris	1782	*Born December 5*
Washington's Farewell Address	1796	*Becomes clerk in law firm of Francis Silvester*
John Adams elected President		
	1800	*Made delegate to the congressional caucus in Troy*
Jefferson inaugurated as President	1801	*Works in New York law office as clerk*
Louisiana Purchase	1803	*Admitted to the bar*
Lewis and Clark expedition		*Becomes law partner of James Van Allen*
	1807	*Marries Hannah Hoes*
Madison elected President	1808	*Appointed surrogate of Columbia County, N.Y.*
War with Great Britain	1812	*Elected to New York State senate*
Washington burned	1814	
Treaty of Ghent		
Battle of New Orleans	1815	*Chosen regent of the University of New York*
Monroe elected President	1816	*Re-elected senator*
		Chosen attorney general of New York
Bank panic and depression	1819	*Wife dies*
		Removed from attorney generalship
Missouri Compromise	1820	
	1821	*Attends third New York State constitutional convention*
		Elected to U.S. Senate
Monroe Doctrine	1823	
	1824	*Supports Crawford for Presidency*
John Quincy Adams elected President	1825	
	1827	*Re-elected senator*
Tariff of Abominations	1828	*Supports Jackson for Presidency*
Jackson elected President		*Elected governor of New York*
	1829	*Appointed Secretary of State*
Antimasonic party established	1831	*Resigns as Secretary of State*
Nullification controversy	1832	*Appointment as minister to Great Britain rejected by Senate*
Jackson vetoes Bank recharter		*Elected Vice President*
Jackson re-elected		

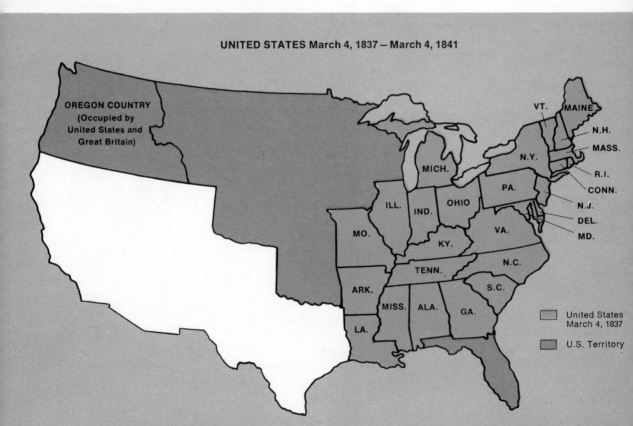

UNITED STATES March 4, 1837 — March 4, 1841

A preview of
VOLUME 4

In the next volume are the life stories of William H. Harrison, hero of Tippecanoe; of John Tyler, who became President when Harrison died; of James K. Polk, who waged a war with Mexico; of "Old Rough-and-Ready" Zachary Taylor; and of the ill-fated Millard Fillmore.

THE AMERICAN HERITAGE BOOK OF THE

4

PRESIDENTS AND FAMOUS AMERICANS

President John Tyler

A campaign flag from the election of 1840

James K. Polk

William Henry Harrison at the Battle of Tippecanoe

DELL

A huge paper ball was rolled from city to city by Harrison supporters in 1840.

The United States won a battle at La Mesa in California during the conflict with Mexico.

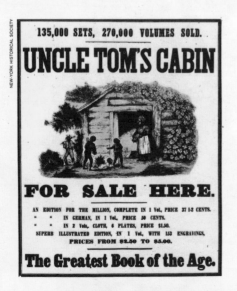

An ad for Harriet Beecher Stowe's book

1.

Which President campaigned on the slogans "All of Oregon, all of Texas" and "54° 40′ or Fight!" In what year was he elected?

2.

"His large head and torso did not match his unusually short legs. A typical uniform for him consisted of baggy cotton pants, a plain coat bearing no insignia, and a farmer's wide-brimmed straw hat. He reviewed his troops or observed a battle's progress seated sideways on his war horse, 'Old Whitey,' with one leg thrown over the pommel of his saddle." To which President does that refer?

3.

Who was the only former President of the United States to serve in the Confederate house of representatives?

4.

Which general, and future unsuccessful presidential candidate, led United States troops into Mexico City in 1847?

5.

"Making the most of the symbol, the Whigs built a network of log cabin campaign headquarters, gave out log cabin songbooks, and dispensed log cabin cider." Which presidential election is being described?

6.

"The fifteen slave states resented abolishment of the slave trade in the District of Columbia and the admission of California as a free state and New Mexico and Utah as territories open to 'popular sovereignty.' The fifteen free states abhorred the provision that declared a runaway slave the private property of his owner, even in a free state." What famous legislation is being described? Which President signed it into law?

7.

"He rose to real greatness on occasion: the brave and patriotic support he gave Tyler; the thundering voice replying to Hayne against nullification; the declaration of allegiance, not to Massachusetts [his home after 1816] . . . but to the Union and the Compromise of 1850." Which American statesman is being described?

8.

Which President fought to have Texas annexed to the Union, and succeeded just three days before his term was over?

This cartoon shows the United States cutting up Mexico with scissors marked "Gen. Taylor."

Above: James K. Polk sits in a fragile house, representing the goals of his administration.

Below: an eagle from a poster praising Taylor

ANSWERS: 1. James K. Polk, 1844 2. Zachary Taylor 3. John Tyler 4. General Winfield Scott 5. William Henry Harrison was the "log cabin candidate" in 1840 6. The Compromise of 1850, signed by President Millard Fillmore 7. Daniel Webster 8. John Tyler

FAMOUS AMERICANS

Included in Volume 4 are Washington Irving, the author of *Rip Van Winkle* and *The Legend of Sleepy Hollow,* who was also an effective American diplomat; Lewis Cass, who fought a losing battle for the Presidency against Zachary Taylor in 1848; George Bancroft, historian and statesman; George Dallas, who fought for the admission of Texas to the United States and later became Polk's Vice President; and the other prominent Americans shown on this page.

Samuel Houston, hero of Texas' fight for freedom from Mexico

Sarah Polk, who forbade wine and dancing in the White House

Daniel Webster, the "golden-voiced" orator and statesman

Brigham Young, who shepherded the Mormons to Utah in 1846

Julia Gardiner Tyler, a beautiful and vivacious First Lady

Whig party formed	1834	
Texas declares independence	1836	*Elected President*
Siege of the Alamo		
Specie Circular issued		
Bank panic and depression	1837	*Fights for Independent Treasury*
Caroline affair	1838	*Issues neutrality proclamation*
Aroostook War	1839	*Sends General Winfield Scott to Maine to negotiate truce*
Harrison elected President	1840	*Independent Treasury established*
		Loses bid for re-election
Tyler becomes President	1841	*Retires to Kinderhook*
Independent Treasury Act repealed		
Webster-Ashburton Treaty	1842	
Polk elected President	1844	*Tries unsuccessfully for Democratic presidential nomination*
Texas annexed	1845	
War with Mexico	1846	
Oregon settlement		
Independent Treasury revived		
Wilmot Proviso		
Treaty of Guadalupe Hidalgo	1848	*Runs unsuccessfully for President on Free-Soil ticket*
Taylor elected President		*Retires*
Compromise of 1850	1850	
Buchanan elected President	1856	
Harpers Ferry	1859	
Lincoln elected President	1860	
Civil War begins	1861	
Battle of Shiloh	1862	*Dies July 24*

BIOGRAPHICAL FACTS

BIRTH: Kinderhook, N.Y., Dec. 5, 1782

ANCESTRY: Dutch

FATHER: Abraham Van Buren; b. Albany, N.Y., Feb. 17, 1737; d. April 8, 1817

FATHER'S OCCUPATION: Farmer

MOTHER: Maria Hoes Van Alen Van Buren; b. 1747; d. Feb. 16, 1817

BROTHERS: Lawrence (1786–1868); Abraham (1788–1836)

SISTERS: Derike (1777–1865); Hannah (1780–?)

HALF BROTHER: James Isaac Van Alen (1776–1870); two others

WIFE: Hannah Hoes; b. Kinderhook, N.Y., March 8, 1783; d. Albany, N.Y., Feb. 5, 1819

MARRIAGE: Kinderhook, N.Y., Feb. 21, 1807

CHILDREN: Abraham (1807–1873); John (1810–1866); Martin (1812–1855); Smith Thompson (1817–1876)

HOME: Lindenwald, Kinderhook, N.Y.

EDUCATION: Village schools; studied in law office

RELIGIOUS AFFILIATION: Dutch Reformed

OCCUPATIONS BEFORE PRESIDENCY: Lawyer; politician

PRE-PRESIDENTIAL OFFICES: Surrogate of Columbia County, N.Y.; New York State Senator; Attorney General of New York; Delegate to Third New York State Constitutional Convention; U.S. Senator; Governor of New York; Secretary of State; Vice President

POLITICAL PARTY: Democratic, during Presidency; Free-Soil, from 1848

AGE AT INAUGURATION: 54

OCCUPATION AFTER PRESIDENCY: Politician

DEATH: Kinderhook, N.Y., July 24, 1862

PLACE OF BURIAL: Kinderhook Cemetery, Kinderhook, N.Y.

ELECTION OF 1836

CANDIDATES	ELECTORAL VOTE	POPULAR VOTE
Martin Van Buren Democratic	170	765,483
William H. Harrison Whig	73	
Hugh L. White Whig	26	739,795
Daniel Webster Whig	14	
Willie P. Mangum Anti-Jacksonian	11	

THE VAN BUREN ADMINISTRATION

INAUGURATION: March 4, 1837; the Capitol, Washington, D.C.

VICE PRESIDENT: Richard M. Johnson

SECRETARY OF STATE: John Forsyth

SECRETARY OF THE TREASURY: Levi Woodbury

SECRETARY OF WAR: Joel R. Poinsett

ATTORNEY GENERAL: Benjamin F. Butler; Felix Grundy (from Sept. 1, 1838); Henry D. Gilpin (from Jan. 11, 1840)

POSTMASTER GENERAL: John M. Niles

SECRETARY OF THE NAVY: Mahlon Dickerson; James K. Paulding (from July 1, 1838)

SUPREME COURT APPOINTMENTS: John Catron (1837); John McKinley (1837); Peter V. Daniel (1841)

25th CONGRESS (March 4, 1837–March 4, 1839):
Senate: 30 Democrats; 18 Whigs; 4 Others
House: 108 Democrats; 107 Whigs; 24 Others

26th CONGRESS (March 4, 1839–March 4, 1841):
Senate: 28 Democrats; 22 Whigs
House: 124 Democrats; 118 Whigs